100 THINGS
BULLS FANS
SHOULD KNOW & DO
BEFORE THEY DIE

Kent McDill

TRIUMPH
BOOKS

Library of Congress Cataloging-in-Publication Data

McDill, Kent.
  100 things Bulls fans should know & do before they die / Kent McDill.
    p. cm.
  ISBN 978-1-60078-650-1
  1. Chicago Bulls (Basketball team)—History—Miscellanea. 2. Basketball teams—Illinois—Chicago—History—Miscellanea. I. Title. II. Title: One hundred things Bulls fans should know and do before they die.
  GV885.52.C45M43 2011
  796.323'640977311—dc23

                                          2011035125

This book is available in quantity at special discounts for your group or organization. For further information, contact:

    Triumph Books LLC
    814 North Franklin Street
    Chicago, Illinois 60610
    (312) 337-0747
    www.triumphbooks.com

Printed in U.S.A.
ISBN: 978-1-60078-650-1
Design by Patricia Frey
All photos courtesy of AP Images unless otherwised noted

To my children—Haley, Dan, Lindsey, and Kyle—for providing me the spark I need every day

Contents

Acknowledgments

I wrote this book alone. The Park Ridge Public Library and the Internet provided me with all of the research materials I needed. The only person I actually bothered for information was Steve Schanwald, the Bulls executive vice president of business operations. But I would like to acknowledge all of the people that I thought about while writing this book. The list includes all of the colleagues from other news sources that I worked with and traveled with from 1988 to 1999 when I was covering the Bulls for the *Daily Herald*. They include Sam Smith, Melissa Isaacson, and Terry Armour of the *Chicago Tribune*; Lacy Banks, Mike Mulligan, Dave Hoekstra, J.A. Adande, and John Jackson of the *Chicago Sun-Times*; and my *Herald* colleagues Mike Imrem, Barry Rozner, and Mike McGraw.

I also want to acknowledge all of the assistance I received while covering the Bulls from the team's media relations staff, including Tim Hallam, Joyce Szymanski, Tom Smithburg, John Diamond, Lori Flores Weisskopf, Sebrina Brewster, Matt Yob, and Shaun Hickombottom.

Thanks to the *Herald* for hiring me to cover the Bulls in the first place, and thanks to the *Herald* for keeping me on the beat through all six championship seasons.

I made great friends while covering the Bulls. This book reminds me of all the good times we had.

Introduction

In spring 2011, I received an invitation to write *100 Things Bulls Fans Should Know & Do Before They Die.* The thinking was that with 11 years as a beat writer for the *Daily Herald* and another decade of Bulls coverage for other entities, it would be a relatively easy assignment.

What did they know?

My first thought was that 100 wasn't enough. I figured that I could write 100 things on Michael Jordan and the six championship teams alone. In fact, I was concerned that the book would turn into yet another tome on the remarkable dynasty of the 1990s.

So I started by writing about other aspects of the Bulls. I went back and investigated the franchise's beginnings. Then I went the other way and studied the way the current Bulls team was built. I came up with about half the book working from either side of the dynasty.

So with half the book left, I started trying to figure out how to tell the incredible story of Michael Jordan, Scottie Pippen, Phil Jackson, and the six-time NBA champion Chicago Bulls of the '90s. As you will see, some stories intermingle with others, but I think the entire story is here for you to enjoy.

Numbering the chapters was the hardest part. How do you decide which championship should be ranked higher: '92 or '93? I know you won't agree with all my rankings, but I've got my reasons for each one.

I think this book does a good job of telling the story of the Chicago Bulls from 1966 to 2012. It was a pleasure to write, and having just re-read it, I think a Bulls fan of any age will get pleasure from it as well.

And now, on to No. 1.

1 Michael Jordan

Nobody knew. If they tell you they knew, they're lying.

When Michael Jordan joined the Chicago Bulls in 1984, he did so with a reputation, but not the reputation he left the team with some 14 years later.

Following his three-year collegiate career at North Carolina, Jordan came to the Bulls with the expectation that he would be a wonderful athlete to watch, a tremendous dunker, a high-flying talent like the Bulls had perhaps never known.

But no one knew about Jordan's relentless competitiveness, at least not to the level he eventually displayed. No one knew that he would be impossible to stop offensively.

In his first season with the Bulls, Jordan averaged 28.2 points and shot over 50 percent from the field. He led the Bulls to the playoffs that first year despite the team having a 38–44 record. The Bulls lost to the Milwaukee Bucks in the first round.

After missing 64 games with a foot injury in his second season, Jordan came back in March '86 and got the Bulls into the playoffs again with a record of 30–52. There they got a first-round matchup against the Boston Celtics. In the second game of the three-game series in Boston, Jordan scored a playoff-record 63 points in a losing effort, giving an indication of who he was in terms of competitiveness and scoring ability. After that game, Hall of Famer Larry Bird compared Jordan to God.

In his third season, completely healthy once again, Jordan really set the NBA on its ear with 37 points per game. He scored more than 3,000 points in the season, something that had not been done since Wilt Chamberlain's heyday. He added more than 200 steals and 100 blocks, playing the entire game on both ends of the court to indicate his status as a complete player.

In the '87–88 season, he won his first MVP award after scoring 35 points per game. He was also named Defensive Player of the Year. The Bulls finished above .500 for the first time with Jordan at 50–32 and won a playoff series for the first time against the Cleveland Cavaliers. They were eliminated in the second round by the Detroit Pistons.

The Bulls were eliminated each of the next two years by the Pistons in the Eastern Conference Finals, but Jordan continued his scoring mastery, averaging well over 30 points a game.

In the '90–91 season, the Bulls finally had the will and the talent to beat the Pistons in the Eastern Conference Finals and went on to defeat the Los Angeles Lakers in the NBA finals for their first title. Jordan's competitiveness and emotional need to win came out in the postgame locker room celebration when he hugged the championship trophy and cried, huddled with his father and best friend, James Jordan.

With one title under his belt, Jordan was unstoppable the next two years. He led the Bulls to the NBA title in '92 in a convincing series against the Portland Trail Blazers, who were led by one of Jordan's so-called athletic predecessors, Clyde Drexler. In '93, Jordan and the Bulls beat the Phoenix Suns in the Finals for their third straight title. He averaged over 40 points in the finals.

After the '93 playoffs, Jordan faced two adversities. He was accused of having a gambling problem, although he never committed any crimes. He also had to deal with the July death of his father, which was believed to be a factor in his decision to retire before the start of the '93–94 season.

Jordan attempted to play professional baseball, the sport that was his first love, but failed to get above Double-A level.

Revitalized by his absence from the game, Jordan returned to the Bulls in the spring of '95, but the Bulls lost to the Orlando Magic

Michael Jordan, 1986 (Getty Images)

in the second round of the playoffs when Jordan was revealed to be slightly out of shape and slow with his reaction times. In the summer of '95, Jordan rededicated himself to the task of an 82-game NBA season, and with Pippen and a new cast of teammates, he led the Bulls to three more NBA titles, playing the Seattle SuperSonics once and the Utah Jazz twice. In 1998, with a battle over a new collective bargaining agreement looming and the prospect of the Bulls breaking up their dynasty, Jordan retired again.

By the end of his career with the Bulls, Jordan had won 10 scoring titles, including seven in a row. He owned the top regular season career scoring average of 30.1 points, and the best playoff career scoring average of 33.4 per game. He made the NBA all-defensive team nine times. He won the NBA regular season MVP award five times, the NBA Finals MVP six times, and was named the NBA All-Star Game MVP three times.

He is generally considered the best to have ever played the game.

72–10: Best Record Ever

In 1972, the Los Angeles Lakers, led by Wilt Chamberlain, won 69 games, setting a record that many thought would never be broken.

The 1995–96 Bulls knew they could challenge the mark if things went their way.

With a newly dedicated and physically imposing Michael Jordan returning after his brief retirement, Scottie Pippen at the top of his career after leading the Bulls without Jordan around, and with the addition of Dennis Rodman, the Bulls appeared capable of winning the franchise's fourth NBA title. With Toni Kukoc on the bench, Steve Kerr aiming for the basket from outside, and Luc Longley and Bill Wennington holding down the middle, the Bulls appeared to have championship material. But no one knew just how dominant they were going to be.

The Bulls started the season with five straight wins, four of them at home. They lost at Orlando in the sixth game of the season, but went 10–1 before falling at Seattle by five points. It was their only loss on the so-called circus trip, in which they played seven games on the West Coast over 12 days.

With a 12–2 record heading into home-heavy December, the Bulls won 13 in a row to go to 23–2. Statistically, they were far ahead of the Lakers' mark. After a December 26 loss at Indiana, the Bulls won an amazing 18 games in a row, nine of them on the road.

At one point in the season, Bulls coach Phil Jackson talked about maybe resting players a game or two at a time in order to keep them fresh for the postseason. The one-season record was not on his mind.

Then came their only bump in the road, back-to-back losses at Denver and at Phoenix. That left them with a record of 41–5, and they needed to go 29–7 to get to 70 wins, thus setting the record.

They went 19–2 over their next 21 to raise their record to 60–7. They needed 10 wins in their final 15, and the record seemed a slam dunk for the Bulls.

They suffered two one-point losses on the way, one at Toronto and a very disappointing one at home against Charlotte, but the Charlotte loss on April 8 left them with a record of 66–9 with seven games to play. Four wins out of the final seven? No problem.

They tied the record at Cleveland on April 14, recording a 98–72 win with ease. They flew home for a night, then took a bus ride from Chicago to Milwaukee for the game that would give them the record.

"History; that's what this is all about," Jordan said on the night before the game.

The Bulls did not play a great game. Jordan and Pippen combined to make only 16 of 46 shots. Jordan had a lackluster 22 points with nine rebounds. The Bulls needed key free throws from Steve Kerr down the stretch to win the game, but they did, 86–80, to become the first team in NBA history to win 70 games in a season.

They beat Detroit two nights later for win No. 71, lost to the Pacers at home by one in their last home game of the regular season, then beat the Washington Bullets by 10 in the season finale for a 72–10 final record, one that many people now believe is an unreachable record.

The Bulls finished the season 39–2 at home and 33–8 on the road. The only team to beat the Bulls twice that season was the Indiana Pacers.

3 Scottie Pippen

Batman needed his Robin.

In the summer of 1987, three years after they selected Michael Jordan in the '84 NBA draft, the Bulls got Scottie Pippen out of the University of Central Arkansas, an NAIA school not known as a hotbed of NBA talent.

Pippen started his career at Central Arkansas as the team manager, and he was a walk-on to the basketball team. He started college as a 6'1" guard, but by the time he graduated, he had grown to 6'7". He averaged 23.6 points per game and shot nearly 60 percent in his senior season.

Bulls general manager Jerry Krause loved nothing more than finding a diamond in the rough. He was determined to get Pippen, and was willing to do whatever it took to get him in the draft.

SCOTTIE PIPPEN

The Chicago Bulls No. 2 all time in games, minutes, field goals, steals, assists, and points, and one of the NBA's 50 greatest players, Scottie Pippen. (Triumph Books collection)

The Bulls had the No. 8 pick in the '87 draft, but Krause found out the Sacramento Kings had their eyes on Pippen with the No. 6 pick. Pippen had played well in pre-draft camps, and Krause no longer had the element of surprise to work with.

Krause made a deal with the Seattle SuperSonics, who had the No. 5 pick, to switch picks, based on the agreement that the deal would be made if the Sonics could not get the athlete they wanted with the No. 5 selection. Apparently, the Sonics wanted Reggie Williams, who was selected by the Los Angeles Clippers with the fourth pick.

So Krause asked the Sonics to select Pippen, then the Bulls took Olden Polynice at No. 8, and the teams traded the players immediately.

Pippen joined the Bulls as a skinny, long-legged, long-armed insecure country kid. Joining a team with a high-profile player like Michael Jordan was a shock to his upbringing, which was about as threadbare an existence as you might think possible in the 20th century. He lived in a very small house in Hamburg, Arkansas, with a disabled father and a severely overworked mother, and many siblings.

Pippen joined the team with another country kid, forward Horace Grant out of Clemson, who was drafted 10th in the '87 draft. The two players grew alongside each other in the fast-paced NBA world.

Over the years, under the direction of defensive-minded assistant coach Johnny Bach and open-minded head coach Phil Jackson, Pippen became one of the best defensive players in the history of the NBA.

He played behind veteran forward Brad Sellers his first year, averaging 7.9 points and 3.8 rebounds a game. He ascended to the starting lineup in the second season, and eventually earned the trust of Jordan. His scoring and rebounding averages increased for four years straight, reaching 21 points and 7.7 rebounds in the '91–92 season.

But Pippen was consistently compared to Jordan as well, and sometimes that had a negative effect upon him. When the Bulls lost to the Detroit Pistons in the Eastern Conference Finals in '90, Pippen struggled in Game 7 because of a severe migraine headache, and Chicago fans criticized him for failing to be as tough as Jordan. His headaches were tied to his vision, and contacts eventually solved that problem. But the Bulls lost Game 7 that year, and Pippen was blamed.

In the '91 NBA Finals, Pippen earned his first moment of true fame. Although 6'9" Magic Johnson of the Los Angeles Lakers was considered a point guard, and Pippen was a small forward, Bulls coach Phil Jackson assigned Pippen to guard Johnson, and Pippen's disruptive defense neutralized Johnson frequently throughout the series.

Eventually, Pippen became a two-time U.S. Olympian and was selected one of the top 50 NBA Players of All Time during the '96–97 season.

Pippen played 17 NBA seasons, including one season with Houston and four with Portland after the Bulls broke up their dynasty team at the conclusion of the '98 season. His career averages were 16.1 points and 6.4 rebounds. His number 33 was retired by the Bulls, and he became a member of the Basketball Hall of Fame in 2010.

1991 World Champions

Historically, the NBA finds its champions in the results of the previous season. In most cases, teams that win titles for the first time preceded their championship seasons by getting close, either by losing in the NBA Finals or losing in their conference finals.

Heading into the 1990–91 NBA season, the Bulls seemed to have paid their dues, with two consecutive appearances in the Eastern Conference Finals. In both cases, the Bulls lost to the Detroit Pistons, in six games in '89 and in seven games in '90.

Minor changes were made to the roster for the '90–91 season. Ed Nealy, Jeff Sanders, and Charles Davis were let go, and the Bulls added longtime Atlanta Hawks forward Cliff Levingston, rookie Scott Williams, and veteran shooting guard Dennis Hopson.

But the core of the team, the starting five, remained the same: shooting guard Michael Jordan, small forward Scottie Pippen, power forward Horace Grant, center Bill Cartwright, and point guard John Paxson. Center Stacey King and point guard B.J. Armstrong were coming into their second year, and shooting guard Craig Hodges remained an outside scoring threat after winning the All-Star Game three-point shooting contest the previous season.

The Bulls figured they needed home-court advantage in the playoffs to best the Pistons if the two teams met again in the playoffs, so they pursued the best record in the East from the start of the season. But the season started off in the worst possible way, with three consecutive losses, two of them at home.

The Bulls won their next three games, taking a 3–3 record on the road for the Circus Trip, the annual two-week excursion into the Western Conference while the circus occupied Chicago Stadium.

The season included nine and 11-game winning streaks, as well as a club-record home winning streak of 26 games, from December 14, 1990, to March 23, 1991. From February 4 to March 20, the Bulls went 20–1, with only a loss at Indiana to mar the streak.

The Bulls won six of their final seven games to finish with a 61–21 record, the first 60-win season in club history. They had the best record in the Eastern Conference. They finished the regular season with a very significant 108–100 win over the Detroit Pistons.

The Bulls started the playoffs with a 3–0 sweep of the New York Knicks, winning Game 1 by 41 points. They had an easy time with the Philadelphia 76ers in the second round, taking that best-of-seven series 4–1.

The series against the Pistons for the Eastern Conference title could not have been more representative of the changing of the guard. The Bulls swept the Pistons, winning the final game 115–94.

The final game was memorable not just for getting the Bulls into the NBA Finals for the first time. Detroit guard Isiah Thomas, a Chicago schoolboy legend, led a group of Pistons off the floor before the final buzzer sounded, walking past the Bulls bench without shaking hands or offering any other sort of acknowledgment.

The Bulls won the NBA Finals against the Los Angeles Lakers 4–1, losing the first game at home 93–91, then winning four straight games, including a Game 3 overtime win at Los Angeles. Bulls coach Phil Jackson earned his stripes by making the decision to place Pippen defensively against Lakers 6'9" point guard Magic Johnson, which disrupted the Lakers, who, like the Pistons, were at the end of their prime.

The Bulls won the final game in Los Angeles and received their trophy inside the visitor's locker room at the Great Western Forum. They had to wait to celebrate with their fans until they got home the next day.

Michael Jordan was the league MVP that year, the MVP of the NBA Finals, made the all-NBA First Team, the All-NBA Defensive First Team, and won his fifth-straight scoring title. Scottie Pippen was named to the league's All-Defensive Second Team, although the votes took place before the Finals were played.

The Bulls were on their way. They were champions, the first major-sport professional champion for the city of Chicago since the 1985 Chicago Bears. And best of all, they were relatively young. The future looked bright.

Dennis Rodman

In 1995, the phrase "his reputation precedes him" applied better to Dennis Rodman than to just about any other person on the planet.

Rodman joined the Bulls at the age of 34 in a trade from San Antonio, where he had played two years and gone through numerous clashes with coaches and star center David Robinson. After spending seven years with the Detroit Pistons and winning two NBA titles, Rodman had allowed his personality to blossom with the Spurs. He began to dye his close-cropped hair and dress to express himself. His self-expression ran onto the basketball court, where he dueled with opponents and teammates alike.

His reputation for loutish behavior ran perpendicular to his reputation as a basketball player. He was unique on the floor as well, with a nose for the ball unlike most players. He was willing to sacrifice his body in order to get his team an extra possession, and while teammates wished he would settle down off the court, they appreciated what he did on it.

Bulls general manager Jerry Krause polled coach Phil Jackson and players Michael Jordan and Scottie Pippen to see if they wanted Rodman on the team. They all gave their blessing to the idea, and Rodman became a Bull.

The trade shocked the world for about half a dozen reasons, chief among them the timing (October 2, 1996, just before the start of training camp) and Rodman's reputation in Chicago (Bulls fans hated him).

One of the hardest-working men in the game, Rodman formed himself into the greatest rebounder of his generation.
(Triumph Books collection)

When the Bulls and Detroit Pistons were playing each other in the playoffs in 1989 through 1991, Rodman was a thorn in the Bulls' side. His offensive rebounding and defense were something the Bulls had to overcome, and they eventually did. But Rodman had also thrown Pippen into a basketball stanchion in a playoff game in '91, giving Pippen a scar he still has. The bad blood seemed lifelong after the Bulls defeated the Pistons on the way to the '91 NBA title.

Instead, cooler heads prevailed and Rodman was allowed to join the team.

"Join" was perhaps the wrong word. He was around, and he did everything the team required of him early on, but he did not work on a relationship with Jordan or Pippen for the first few months.

"I have not had a conversation with Dennis," Pippen said at one point during the first season. "I've never had a conversation with Dennis in my life."

Jordan had a different take on Rodman. The two men were clearly never going to be friends; Rodman was completely different from Jordan. But Jordan realized Rodman was going to help him win another title.

A couple of months before joining the team, Rodman had appeared in a wedding dress in New York at a book signing. He continued to test everyone in regards to his sexual orientation with his dress, although he also continued to make news with the women he dated, including model Carmen Electra, whom he married for 10 days.

In his first season with the Bulls, Rodman won another rebounding title, played the kind of defense he was best known for, and developed an on-court relationship with both Jordan and Pippen. The NBA All-Defensive team for the '95–96 season included all three star Bulls players.

To list all his transgressions during that season would require a separate book. The highlight—or lowlight—of the '95–96 season was when he head-butted a referee in a game in New Jersey, earning a six-game suspension from the NBA.

In the playoffs his first year with the Bulls he averaged 13.7 rebounds per game. In the finals against Seattle, he grabbed 20 rebounds in one game and tied an NBA record with 11 offensive boards. In another game, he had 19 rebounds.

The Bulls won the title again in '96–97 with Rodman earning yet another NBA rebounding title, his sixth consecutive. But he got in trouble again, with the best story being the night he fell into the front row of cameramen in pursuit of a loose ball and then kicked a cameraman in the groin. He was suspended for 11 games for that indiscretion, and paid the man $200,000.

The '97–98 season was more of the same, with Rodman winning another rebounding title, having a 29-rebound game during the regular season, and venturing into the world of professional wrestling during the season.

After every game, Rodman gave his jersey away to a fan in the stands.

After the '98 season, the NBA had a temporary work stoppage due to the collective bargaining agreement between players and owners, and Rodman did not play again for the Bulls. But his three years with the team were so successful that fans tried heartily to get the team to consider retiring his No. 91 jersey.

1996 World Champions

When the Bulls were dismissed from the 1995 playoffs by the Orlando Magic, Michael Jordan realized his return to the NBA from his premature retirement was itself premature. He wasn't in the shape he needed to be in to play, especially at his now advanced age of 32 years old.

So during the summer Jordan worked harder than he ever had in order to prepare himself for the upcoming season. After all, the writing was on the wall: the Bulls were in good shape to win yet another NBA title.

After all, they would have Jordan, and they would have Scottie Pippen, who had grown up in the year and a half he played without Jordan. He was now clearly not only one of the best players in the game, but one of the best to ever play the game. Jordan and Pippen would combine to present a defensive front few teams could penetrate.

And they had Toni Kukoc, the Croatian sensation who had already spent two years with the team after coming over from Italy in the hopes of playing with Jordan. Those dreams were now realized, and he was ready to be a contributor as well.

Just like they did during the first three-peat, the Bulls had their three-headed monster at center. They had Luc Longley, Bill Wennington, and Will Perdue to play the middle.

Bulls general manager Jerry Krause had been building the framework for a new championship even before Jordan came back. His bench included outside shooting–threat Steve Kerr; hard-working forward Jud Buechler; and guard Ron Harper, who was the Bulls' starting shooting guard before Jordan returned.

Then, the NBA world was turned upside-down in October when the Bulls traded Perdue to San Antonio and acquired forward Dennis Rodman, the former Detroit Piston Bulls fans loved to hate. Rodman, who by '95 was a cross-dressing, freedom-loving, rebounding machine, was set to make the Bulls a powerhouse beyond any previous reckoning.

And that is who they were. They set an NBA record by going 72–10. They became the NBA equivalent of the Beatles. Their popularity was impossible to imagine. There was simply nothing in the American sports world to compare.

On the same day the Bulls announced the acquisition of Rodman, they also announced the signing of backup point guard Randy Brown, who had played four years in Sacramento. Although his signing got little attention because of Rodman's presence, he became the first player from Chicago that Krause ever signed. Krause believed family and friend distractions would negatively affect any player who grew up in the Windy City, but he made an exception for Brown.

The Bulls' cruise through the regular season gave rise to the idea they would cruise through the playoffs. But they had to play the games.

Part of the story surrounding the Bulls dynasty years is that there were so many subplots, and one came up in '96 when Pat Riley became coach of the Miami Heat. Riley and Bulls coach Phil Jackson had developed a true dislike for each other when the earlier Bulls played Riley's New York Knicks, and the dislike would fester again in the '96 playoff opening round series.

Perhaps the most interesting aspect of that first round series, which the Bulls swept in three games, was the mind games between Rodman and Alonzo Mourning, the Heat's All-Star center. Mourning was reputed to be a homophobe, and it was clear that he did not take well to Rodman's occasional forays into cross-dressing and gender-bending concepts. So during one game, when Rodman lined up next to Mourning during a teammate's free throw, Rodman patted Mourning on the butt, something athletes often do to other athletes.

But this butt slap clearly rattled Mourning, and Rodman delighted in the moment.

The Bulls beat the New York Knicks in the second round, losing only one game. They then swept Shaquille O'Neal's Orlando

Magic in the Eastern Conference Finals as payback for beating the Bulls in the '95 playoffs.

That set up a final against the Seattle SuperSonics, who were led by power forward Shawn Kemp and point guard Gary Payton. The Bulls needed six games, but won the championship at home, this time before an adoring crowd at the United Center, which was enjoying its first NBA title.

In his comeback season, Jordan won the league's scoring title, averaging 30.4 points per game. It was his eighth NBA scoring crown. He was named regular season MVP, All-Star MVP, and Finals MVP. Dennis Rodman won his fifth consecutive rebounding title. Jordan and Pippen were named to the All-NBA First Team, and Jordan, Pippen, and Rodman were named to the All-NBA Defensive First Team, taking three of the five spots.

Although he wasn't happy about it, Toni Kukoc was named the league's Sixth Man of the Year. Phil Jackson earned NBA Coach of the Year honors, and Jerry Krause was selected Executive of the Year, which was obviously well deserved.

The '95–96 Bulls were the best team the NBA had ever seen.

7 Chicago Stadium

Built at the height of the depression in 1929, Chicago Stadium was known as "The Old Barn" until it later became known as the "Madhouse on Madison." It served as the home to the Chicago Bulls from their inception in 1967 to 1994. It was located on the city's near west side.

Super Fan

The Bulls never shied away from ways to gain attention, and they found one by accident.

During the 1970s, when the Bulls were warming to the Chicago Stadium and the city was warming to the success of the Bulls, a man named Jeff Platt started a tradition of running around the stadium floor in the aisle between the bench seats and the first row of spectator seats. The sporting-goods salesman would wave his arms and slap fives with the fans at the first level, attempting to get the crowd into the contest and back the Bulls.

Platt was fat, but he could run. He wore a Bulls T-shirt to games, and once fans came to realize he was going to do this time and again, he became popular and was known as Super Fan.

Platt is not to be confused with the Superfans, the comedy troupe that made fun of Chicago accents and really, really liked Bears coach Mike Ditka (see "Superfans" chapter).

The building was owned by Arthur Wirtz, owner of the Chicago Blackhawks. When the Bulls entered the NBA, he invited them to play at the Stadium so the building would have fewer empty evenings.

Somehow, the building made noise even when it was empty. When it was filled with fans for either the Chicago Blackhawks or the Chicago Bulls the noise cascaded from the dangerously tilted upper-tier seats down to the floor, creating a deafening cacophony of sounds from both the people and the structure.

When the Bulls got their start, however, and first moved into the building after a season at the Chicago Amphitheatre, the building also produced thunderous echoes. With few people in the stands, the sound of a bouncing basketball itself bounced around the interior.

Although the basketball and hockey floors were on the first floor of the building, there was a basement, where the very small locker rooms and training facilities were. Athletes had to climb the

22 stairs to get to the arena, including the Blackhawks and their opponents in their skates.

Because the team colors for both home teams were black and red, the entire interior was painted in black and red and was very dark.

The Stadium was host to the Bulls' first three championship teams, although they only won the second title in the building. After winning Game 6 against the Portland Trail Blazers, the team retired to the basement locker room but returned after a few minutes to celebrate the victory with the fans still waiting in the arena.

The Stadium hosted other championship games, including the first-ever NFL title game held indoors. That was in 1932, when weather forced the game between the Chicago Bears and Portsmouth Spartans into the building. Dirt was brought into the building to simulate a football field, and the Bears won the game 9–0.

In 1988, the Stadium hosted the NBA All-Star Game and the weekend festivities, which included Michael Jordan's famous and controversial Slam Dunk Contest win over Dominique Wilkins.

The final event at the Stadium was a charity basketball game hosted by Bulls forward Scottie Pippen. Michael Jordan had retired the year before and had become a minor league baseball player, but he played in the game and scored 52 points. At the conclusion of the game, Jordan knelt at center court and kissed the Chicago Bulls logo.

The Stadium was demolished in '95 and is now the site of a parking lot used for the United Center, which is now home to the Bulls and Blackhawks. Many fans gathered and cried as the building was brought down. Bricks from the structure were sold to fans after the demolition.

A plaque reading "Chicago Stadium 1929–1994, remember the roar" is located on the north side of the United Center.

8 The United Center

"The House that Jordan Built" is the name given to the United Center, which is also known by most fans as "The UC." It was completed in 1995 after Chicago Stadium was deemed inadequate for the needs of the Bulls and Blackhawks, specifically in the area of luxury suites for maximum revenue.

The United Center was built on the south side of Madison Street, across the street from where Chicago Stadium stood from 1929 to 1994. The UC retained the "Madhouse on Madison" moniker thanks to its location.

By the time the mid-'90s rolled around, the Bulls were owned by a group of investors led by Jerry Reinsdorf, and they shared the cost of the new building with the Blackhawks owners. Their goal was to maximize revenue by including two levels of luxury boxes for corporate groups or other forms of high rollers. It created an upper level of seats, known as "the nose-bleed seats," at the 500 level.

The building was designed with scientifically enhanced acoustics in an attempt to duplicate the noise that poured down upon the floor at Chicago Stadium.

The United Center is home to the most famous depiction of Michael Jordan's career, the statue known as "The Spirit," which depicts Jordan rising above an opponent for one of his trademark dunks. It is on the east side of the stadium in front of the team offices.

Soon after the building was opened, Jordan returned from his first retirement and eventually led the Bulls to three more titles, in '96, '97, and '98. Unlike Chicago Stadium, which only got to host one championship game for the Bulls, the UC was host to two, in '96 against Seattle and in '97 against Utah.

Chicago Stadium (foreground) is shown in 1993 as construction continues on the United Center (background).

The newness of the United Center provided not just increased revenues but increased space. On the concourses that ring the outside of the seating area, the Bulls have two musical groups perform on the first and third levels before every game. There are bars and restaurants throughout the arena as well.

The Bulls have a large locker room with anterooms on either side. There are offices for the coach and assistant coaches, and rooms for the full array of medical and video equipment professional teams require.

In the United Center rafters hang banners for all of the Bulls' and Blackhawks' greatest players and accomplishments. The Bulls have retired jersey numbers: 4 for Jerry Sloan, 10 for Bob Love, 23 for Michael Jordan, and 33 for Scottie Pippen. They also have banners raised for coach Phil Jackson, who coached the Bulls to six titles, and general manager Jerry Krause, who built the teams that won the titles. There are also Bulls banners for seven division titles, six conference titles, and six NBA championships.

The banner for the division title in '96 has a banner attached below signifying the fact the team won a record 72 games that season.

The Blackhawks have banners for seven retired player jersey numbers, 14 division champions, four conference champions, and four Stanley Cup champions.

On May 17, 2011, the United Center hosted the last show for the long-running *Oprah Winfrey Show*, a celebration that Michael Jordan attended. The date of the show was a Tuesday, and since the producers needed all day the previous Monday to prepare for the show, the dates for the '10–11 Eastern Conference Finals series between the Bulls and Miami Heat had to be altered.

Jerry Krause

There are not a lot of front-office personnel with their names up in banners at NBA stadiums, especially ones who never played the game of basketball.

Jerry Krause is one of them.

Krause was the Bulls general manager who put together the teams that helped Michael Jordan win six NBA championships in the 1990s.

While arguments will go on forever over the amount of influence Krause had on the team's winning ways, there is little argument that he found the players and coaches who could complement Jordan in such a way that they could create one of basketball's greatest dynasties.

Krause is a legendary figure in Bulls history, and like most legendary figures, his story goes way back.

Krause was with the Bulls almost from the beginning. He was brought in as a scout in the late '60s. He clashed with the Bulls' notoriously feisty coach Dick Motta and left the organization, but was brought back after Motta left the team in 1976. Krause was named director of player personnel for '76, but left the team a few months later in a dispute over whether he invited Ray Meyer of DePaul to be head coach of the Bulls to replace Motta.

After leaving the Bulls again, Krause began working as a baseball scout for the Chicago White Sox, where he got to know White Sox owner Jerry Reinsdorf.

In 1984, Jerry Reinsdorf and a group of investors purchased a majority stake in the Bulls, and Reinsdorf immediately fired Rod Thorn and promoted Krause to VP of basketball operations.

Krause, a lifelong scout and gym junkie, had finally made it to the big leagues.

Krause was not responsible for Michael Jordan being on the team (a fact that got in his way his entire career with the Bulls), but he was charged with finding players who could play with Jordan.

Over the years, Krause engineered a number of deals that benefited the Bulls. He drafted Charles Oakley out of tiny Virginia Union, then traded the popular power forward for center Bill Cartwright, a cornerstone of the first Bulls three-peat.

He figured out a way to get Scottie Pippen in the '87 NBA draft, working out a deal with Seattle in which they traded the players they initially drafted (the history books say the Bulls drafted Olden Polynice, which is true, but they immediately traded him for Pippen). He drafted Horace Grant along with Pippen, thus finding two-fifths of the starting lineup for the first three-peat in one day.

The Cartwright deal in the summer of 1988 was seen as folly, but turned out to be a great way for the Bulls to solidify their center position. Krause drafted B.J. Armstrong and Stacey King in '89, and they became two key members of the championship bench.

Then Krause located the others through draft, trade, or free agent pickup, for all six NBA championship teams: John Paxson, Craig Hodges, Cliff Levingston, Scott Williams, Will Perdue, Dennis Hopson, Bobby Hansen, Trent Tucker, and Darrell Walker.

He hired Doug Collins as his first coach, turning the team over to him in '86. In '87, he pulled Phil Jackson out of the Continental Basketball Association and made him an assistant coach.

By the time the '90s rolled around, Krause had made one enemy: Michael Jordan. Jordan did not like the fact that Krause traded his best friend on the team, Charles Oakley, for Bill Cartwright, a player to whom Jordan never warmed up.

But the Bulls won the '91 NBA title, and two more after that, and Krause was seen as a team-building genius.

High schoolers Tyson Chandler and Eddy Curry hold up their jerseys after being drafted by the Bulls in 2001.

In the summer of '90, Krause, who became known as "The Sleuth" for his ways of digging up unknown basketball talent, reached across the Atlantic for his next basketball find. He drafted Toni Kukoc, a star forward with the Yugoslavian (and then Croatian) basketball team, an international powerhouse. But Kukoc, wary of moving to the United States, did not sign with the team until the summer of '93.

Finally, Kukoc agreed to join the Bulls, but soon thereafter, Jordan announced his retirement in August. Krause had to start a rebuilding program.

Krause had already acquired center Luc Longley for Stacey King. He signed Bill Wennington, Steve Kerr, Jud Buechler, and Ron Harper for his new-look Bulls. Then Jordan came back in the spring of '95.

Suddenly, Krause had to think about an immediate championship team, and he engineered one of the most amazing trades in Bulls history, sending Will Perdue to San Antonio for Dennis Rodman, a player hated in Chicago for his time with the Detroit Pistons back in the early '90s. But Rodman's inclusion on the team created a club that went 72–10 in '95–96 and went on to win three more titles.

A bad relationship with Jackson, a player strike, and other issues caused Jordan to retire again in '98 and Jackson to leave the team. The following years did not go well for Krause, although he did draft Elton Brand, whom he unfortunately traded in order to pick Tyson Chandler and Eddie Curry in the 2001 NBA draft.

Krause had difficulty replacing Jordan and Jackson, as might be expected. But because Krause had had difficulty with his relationships with the Chicago media, his difficulties were seen as failures. He resigned as the Bulls vice president of player personnel in '03.

10 Phil Jackson

While playing with the New York Knicks in the mid-1970s, Phil Jackson wrote a book titled *Maverick*. It was a description of him and his lifelong struggle to be a little bit unique in the cookie-cutter world of professional basketball.

Unlike so many other pro athletes, who predominantly come from urban upbringings, Jackson was from Montana. He played college ball at the University of North Dakota, an NCAA Division II school. He was an All-American there, a 6'8" phenom with good post moves and a great defensive ability.

After a pro career that included two NBA championships with the New York Knicks, Jackson became an assistant coach with the New Jersey Nets, then switched to the broadcast booth. His first head coaching job was with the Albany Patroons of the Continental Basketball Association, a team he led to the CBA title in 1984. He had moved on to a CBA team in Puerto Rico when Bulls general manager Jerry Krause thought he would be a good choice to serve as an assistant coach with Doug Collins, who already had two aging assistants in Johnny Bach and Tex Winter.

When Krause and owner Jerry Reinsdorf decided Doug Collins was not going to be able to coach the Bulls to an NBA title, they turned to Jackson, who was 43 years old at the time he was hired to coach the Bulls for the '89–90 season. Jackson was being handed the reins of a team that had advanced to the Eastern Conference Finals and was clearly on the rise.

One of Jackson's first decisions was to fully integrate Tex Winter's triple-post offense into the Bulls' scheme. The complicated offense required players to know exactly where they were to be on the floor and what their options were in every possession, and required severe coaching and time elements. That's why no one had adopted it full scale before. But Jackson saw it as the ultimate team offense, and the Bulls won six titles with it.

Jackson later used the same offense in winning five titles with the Los Angeles Lakers.

Jackson was known for having whipping boys when he coached the Bulls. First it was Horace Grant, who was the third guy in the star lineup that included Michael Jordan and Scottie

Coach Phil Jackson, who as of 2012 has 13 NBA championship rings. Two from his playing days with the Knicks, and the other 11 are as a head coach (six with the Bulls and five with the Lakers). (Triumph Books collection)

Pippen. Later, Jackson picked on Toni Kukoc, who was not only the third guy in terms of star power on the team, but was also a key signing by Krause, who by then had worn thin on the popular head coach.

As the dynasty wore down in the late '90s, Jackson spoke frequently about leaving the team. When the Bulls won the title in '98 and there was talk of a work stoppage because of negotiations over a new collective bargaining agreement between the NBA and the players union, Jackson officially resigned from the Bulls. His relationship with Krause had soured significantly, and it became evident it was time to move on.

Jackson eventually became the winningest coach in NBA history in terms of total titles and entered the Hall of Fame in 2007.

11 The 1984 NBA Draft

In 1984, the NBA draft consisted of 10 rounds, with 23 teams in the league at the time. The draft order was determined by the previous year's record, with the worst team in each conference getting a shot at the No. 1 pick. The Houston Rockets were the worst team in the Western Conference and the Indiana Pacers were the worst team in the Eastern Conference, so they flipped a coin for the No. 1 pick, which went to the Rockets. The Pacers' selection had already been traded away to the Portland Trail Blazers, who ended up with the second pick. Following a 27–55 season, the Chicago Bulls were choosing third.

Michael Jordan of North Carolina was the Wooden Award winner as the College Player of the Year in 1984 as a junior, and was one of five underclassmen who declared themselves eligible for the NBA draft. One of the others was seven-foot University of Houston center Akeem Olajuwon, who was a natural local hero pick for the Rockets.

The Rockets already had former Virginia center Ralph Sampson, but thought an Olajuwon-Sampson pairing in the middle would make them unbeatable.

The Trail Blazers, coming off a 48–34 season, considered choosing Jordan, but they already had two shooting guards on the roster, all-star veteran Jim Paxson and young high-flyer Clyde Drexler, who was Olajuwon's teammate at Houston. So the Trail Blazers followed the well-known NBA scout edict that you can't coach height, and selected University of Kentucky center Sam Bowie, a reed-thin 7'1" center with a history of leg injuries.

With the third pick, the Bulls jumped at the chance to select Jordan, believing they were getting the best athlete in the draft and a potential star in the NBA. But they did not know they were getting the player who would one day be considered the best player in NBA history.

In fact, when he was drafted, there were questions about whether Jordan could shoot well enough from outside to cause defenses to come out to him and open up the middle. There was thinking that Jordan should play small forward instead of shooting guard, but his height and slight build raised questions.

Jordan made the Bulls braintrust look like geniuses, though. He won the NBA's Rookie of the Year award and was named to the All-NBA Second Team, a surprising selection for a rookie. He ended his career with six NBA championships, was named MVP five times, and was named Defensive Player of the Year once. For comparison, Olajuwon won two NBA titles with the Rockets (but neither while Jordan played full seasons), was named the league's MVP once, and the Defensive Player of the Year twice. Both players ended up in the Basketball Hall of Fame.

Bowie played 10 years in the NBA but had five leg surgeries in that time. He averaged 10.9 points and 7.5 rebounds but played only 139 games in his first five seasons (an average of 28 games a season).

That draft included two other eventual Hall of Famers: Charles Barkley (selected fifth by the Philadelphia 76ers) and John Stockton (selected 16th by the Utah Jazz).

Fans who don't know the details are always amazed to find out Jordan was not the No. 1 pick in the draft the year he came out. They are further amazed to find out he wasn't even No. 2. But the facts of the day seemed just as clear then as they seem amazingly confusing today.

12 Jordan's Rookie Season—1985

As a rookie, the only pressure that existed for Michael Jordan was that which came with his pre-draft hype. He wasn't expected to take the Bulls to the NBA Finals by himself.

But what Jordan did in his first season in the NBA was legendary.

With an amazing array of dunks and athletic moves to the basket, Jordan averaged 28.2 points and shot 52 percent from the field. He hit 84.5 percent of his free throws. He at times appeared unstoppable by the usual NBA defenses.

In the third game of his career, Jordan scored 37 points against the Milwaukee Bucks. Two weeks later, in his ninth game, Jordan scored 45 points. He had four more 40-point-plus games by the time the All-Star break came around. Against Denver, he had 35 points, 15 assists, and 14 rebounds for his first career triple-double in a game won by the Bulls 122–113.

There was no question Jordan was going to be the Bulls' first All-Star since Reggie Theus in 1983. The game was played in Indianapolis, and the hoopla surrounding Jordan's appearance was unlike anything the NBA had seen in recent memory.

But the game became legendary not because of what Jordan did, but because of what Jordan was not allowed to do. For never-disclosed reasons, it seemed like Jordan was denied the ball by his own Eastern Conference teammates, and he finished with seven points on two-for-nine shooting in 22 minutes played.

It was believed that Detroit Pistons guard Isiah Thomas (previously the hero of Chicago basketball fans from his high school days) directed the so-called "freeze-out" of Jordan. Thomas and

Jordan were the starting guards for the East squad. The freeze-out was never proven or admitted to, but the perception is that Thomas was jealous of the attention Jordan was receiving as a yet-unproven star in the league.

Jordan's style of play was reminiscent of Atlanta Hawks forward Dominique Wilkins, with his acrobatic style and smooth approach to the game. But, in the second half of the season, an historic event was about to take place that was going to elevate Jordan to a new level of stardom.

In early 1985, the struggling athletic apparel company Nike signed Jordan to a $2.5 million deal for five years to place his name on a new shoe. The Air Jordan shoe, predominantly red and black, was the biggest hit in athletic shoewear ever. It was the start of an endorsement empire that marked Jordan's entire athletic career. He personally placed Nike at the top of the corporate heap.

Jordan began to wear the shoe immediately in games, but the NBA said it violated league policy because it was not primarily white. They fined Jordan $5,000 per game for wearing it, and he just kept playing in it and paying the fine.

The Bulls finished the first Jordan year with a record of 38–44 and made the playoffs for the first time since 1981. They were eliminated in the first round of the playoffs by the Milwaukee Bucks.

Jordan finished his rookie season setting club records for points scored (2,313), field goals and free throws made, and steals (196). With his 28.2 points per game he finished third in the league in scoring, with Bernard King leading the league with 32.9 points per game. Larry Bird of the Boston Celtics was voted the MVP that year.

13 1998 World Champions

The third year of the second three-peat almost didn't take place.

Phil Jackson, Michael Jordan, and Dennis Rodman were operating on one-year contracts. Jackson, tired of his relationship with Bulls general manager Jerry Krause, was ready to leave the Bulls and move on to the next stage of his life. Jordan was always worried about getting paid what he was worth, and Rodman was seemingly always an experiment that could go horribly wrong. Meanwhile, Scottie Pippen was waiting for his big payday to take place as well.

In the summer of '97, the Bulls were the perfect example that there is such a thing as too much success. But all of the ingredients came together one last time. All parties agreed that the team was simply too good to break up, and the team got together to play the '97–98 season and defend the two previous championships.

Pippen started the season on the injured reserve list with leg problems, and he played only 44 games in the regular season. The Bulls started the season playing like a tired and uninspired team, going 4–4 through their first eight games, and were only 6–4 before starting their usual November road trip.

After losing at Phoenix to drop to 6–5, the Bulls headed to Los Angeles to play the Clippers. Before that game, Pippen, who was still not playing, told a reporter he had played his last game as a Bull, that he was going to demand a trade because the team was not prepared to give him the extension he was looking for. The story became national news, but Pippen eventually came back to the team when he got healthy again.

Unlike previous championship seasons, the Bulls never got on a big run through the NBA until late in the season. With Pippen healthy, the Bulls won 13 straight games through March and April, enough to win the Central Division.

The Bulls won only 62 games in '97-98, which was still a huge number, but not like the 72 and 69 they had won the two previous seasons. They ended up tied with the Utah Jazz for best record in the league, and they were only four games better than the Indiana Pacers in the Central Division of the Eastern Conference.

The Bulls had almost the same roster that they had used the two previous seasons, but again changed backup centers, calling on Joe Kleine to serve as the third center behind Luc Longley and Bill Wennington. They had the same 11 other players from the previous two years, a level of consistency that was unusual, but served them well when they needed it.

The Bulls swept the New Jersey Nets in three games in the opening round and beat the Charlotte Hornets 4–1 in the second round. That set up an Eastern Conference Finals against Reggie Miller and the Indiana Pacers. This ho-hum playoff run was about to get *very* interesting.

Among the many facts about which the Bulls were particularly proud was that they had rarely needed seven games to win a playoff series on the way to an NBA title. Even in the championship round, they dispatched opponents before the final possible game. They beat the Lakers in five games in '91, the Trail Blazers in six games in '92, the Phoenix Suns in six in '93 (even though the Suns had home-court advantage), the SuperSonics in six in '96, and the Jazz in six in '97.

That all changed when they came up against the Pacers.

During the regular season, the Bulls had split four games with the Pacers, and each team had won on the other's home court. The series promised to be good, and Bulls fans were actually worried that it might be too good, from a competitive standpoint.

Chicago held serve in the first two games at the United Center, but the Pacers did the same at Market Square Arena in Indianapolis, winning both games by two points. The Bulls won Game 5 at the UC by 19 points and appeared ready to assume their role once again in the NBA Finals with a Game 6 win in Indianapolis.

Instead, the Pacers pulled off a three-point win, forcing a Game 7. The Bulls won the deciding contest by five points at the UC to advance to the NBA Finals for a rematch against John Stockton, Karl Malone, and the Utah Jazz.

During the regular season, the Bulls played the Jazz twice in 11 days. They lost at home on January 25 against Utah 101–94, when Malone outscored Jordan 35–32, then lost again in Salt Lake City on February 4 101–93, with Jordan getting 40 to Malone's 30.

So the Jazz had home-court advantage, the first time that had happened to the Bulls since the '93 series against the Suns. The teams split the first two games at the Delta Center, then the Bulls won two games at home to go up 3–1 in the best-of-seven series. The Bulls won Game 3 by the unbelievable score of 96–54.

But Utah found its heart again in Game 5 and beat the Bulls at the UC by two points, forcing a trip back to Salt Lake City. In Game 6, the Bulls beat the Jazz 87–86 on a last-second jumper by Jordan and the franchise had its second three-peat.

Jordan won his 10th scoring title that year, averaging 28.7 points per game. He was the league MVP for the fifth time. Rodman collected his seventh consecutive rebounding title (achieved with three different teams).

The minute the final game of the Finals was over, there was a sense that the franchise's decade of dominance was about to end.

14 The Introductions

There was certainly a sense that the Bulls were headed toward an NBA championship. With the selection of Michael Jordan in 1984 and the addition of Scottie Pippen and Horace Grant in '87, the Bulls were on the brink of greatness.

Steve Schanwald, the Bulls vice president of marketing and broadcasting, wanted to celebrate the team in a way no other team had been celebrated. So he created an introduction to the game that has been impersonated (and sometimes directly copied) ever since.

After the visiting team is introduced, the lights at Chicago Stadium (pre-'94) or United Center (post-'94) would dim, and the music would start. The song was "Sirius" by Alan Parsons Project, and today it evokes the memory of one of the greatest teams in NBA history.

Simultaneously with the start of the song, laser lights began to flash around the arena, eventually coming together to focus on center court, where an image of the Bulls logo, the head of Benny the Bull, appears.

The Bulls, by the way, were the first NBA team to dim the stadium lights for introductions. It is a process now used throughout the league, and is made easier with today's new stadiums and their sound and lighting technologies.

During the dynasty years, the visiting team was introduced to the sounds of the song "On the Run" from Pink Floyd's historic album *Dark Side of the Moon*. That tradition was changed in the new century and the visitors are now introduced to the sounds of the "Imperial March" music from Star Wars, a song associated with one of the most hated villains in film history, Darth Vader.

At Chicago Stadium, there was no video board to use. The scoreboard above the floor was old school, with a board on each side to give you lighted messages. At the United Center, the start of the introductions is marked by a digital animation video showing the attack of a number of bulls (the animals) charging through the city of Chicago before reaching the United Center, blasting through the bus of the opposing team for that night's game.

For years, the introductions were done by the public address announcer Ray Clay, and the first words you would hear him say were "And now, *your* Chicago Bulls!"

Through the Jordan years, Clay would introduce the other starters before getting to the star. He would then say the words, "From North Carolina…" and the fans, who were already screaming, turned the volume up a couple of notches, creating more noise than seemingly possible.

The Chicago Stadium, known as The Barn for years and years, was a brick and wood construction, and it seemed to make noise even when empty. When the thousands of fans filled the place and the introductions began, the noise seemed to drop from the upper-deck seats and pound the center of the floor. Sitting at floor level was like being front and center for a rock concert.

By the time the team moved to the United Center, the Bulls staff had the magic of modern technology at its disposal. Reportedly, the building has acoustics that allow the sound that reaches the rafters to be directed back again to the floor, creating the kind of sound level the Stadium was able to produce on its own.

Within a short period of time, the Bulls introductions were mimicked by most of the other teams in the league. Different song, different words, certainly different names, but the effect was similar.

Not the same, though. Nothing could be the same.

15 The Bulls Get Their Start

The NBA dates its existence back to 1946. The Chicago Stags won the Western Division that year but lost in the finals to the Philadelphia Warriors. But the Stags folded in 1950, and Chicago went unrepresented in the league until 1961, when the Chicago Packers entered the league. After the '62–63 season, the Packers (who became the Zephyrs for one year) moved to Baltimore to become the Bullets.

A man named Dick Klein, who had played baseball and basketball at Northwestern University in Evanston, Illinois, and had played professional basketball for a pre-NBA team known as the Chicago Gears, had tried to put together the money to keep the Stags/Zephyrs in Chicago but failed. For the next three years, Klein worked hard to build a group that would put up the money to buy an expansion franchise in the struggling NBA, which desperately wanted a team in Chicago.

Eventually, Klein's group managed to pay the $1.25 million franchise fee needed to get into the league, and the Chicago Bulls were born. The bid for a team was boosted by the American Broadcasting Corporation (ABC) which was negotiating broadcast rights with the league and stated that the broadcast rights would be more valuable with a Chicago team in the league.

The team name came out of Chicago's history as a meat-packing town, a cow town. The Chicago Cows would not have been very menacing, but Klein wanted a one-syllable name to go with the team's existing franchises like the Bears, Cubs, (White) Sox, and (Black) Hawks. Cows was out, but Bulls was in.

The first coach of the Bulls was local hero Johnny "Red" Kerr, a high school legend from Tilden High School and the University of Illinois. Klein initially contacted DePaul University coach Ray

The Bulls Logo

Once the owners of the new NBA franchise came up with the name for the team, it was time to come up with something to visually signify the name. They needed a logo that showed a fierce, wild bull. According to Dick Klein, the first owner of the Bulls, a man named Dean Wessel designed the logo, which was one of about 40 different attempts he made to get what Klein wanted.

"I wanted the Bull to be a true bull, in a bull fight," Klein said in the book *And Now Your Chicago Bulls* by Roland Lazenby. "He's a big and black thing with long horns and red eyes and mean. I wanted a mean-looking Bull. I said 'I want a face.' Then Dean gave me a face that looked real good."

Klein then asked for red eyes and blood somewhere. The Bull he got, which has stayed almost the same from the start of the franchise, is in fact an angry Bull face staring straight ahead, with blood on the tips of the horns. The Bull is glowering, definitely not happy with whoever is looking at him.

The words "Chicago Bulls" are above the bull head, placed inside the tipped bull's horns as if the words are in parentheses.

As of 2012, only four other NBA logos show the full frontal face of the mascot. They are the Minnesota Timberwolves, the Memphis Grizzlies, the Dallas Mavericks (the horse's head is slightly turned), and the Milwaukee Bucks.

The logo does not appear on the jersey, but it is on both sides of the shorts in a triangle on the hip.

Meyer about the job, but Meyer had no interest in leaving the school.

Kerr had played 12 years in the NBA for several teams, most notably the Syracuse Nationals. He was well-known in Chicago as one of the first high school players to make it in the pros, and he had a lot of connections that the team could use for investment purposes.

For financial and contract reasons, Klein selected Kerr in the league's expansion draft out of Baltimore as a player, even though

Kerr was planning to retire from playing. Other players selected were Jerry Sloan from the Bullets, Bob Boozer from the Los Angeles Lakers, and Jim Washington from the St. Louis Hawks. In the college draft, the Bulls first selected Dave Schellhase from nearby Purdue University. He was the top collegiate scorer the previous season.

The Bulls played their initial season in the Chicago Amphitheatre, an old barn of a facility on the city's near south side.

The starting lineup for the first Chicago Bulls game was Sloan and Guy Rodgers at guard, and a front line of Len Chappell, Don Kojis, and Bob Boozer. The upstart Bulls won their first three games, but reality struck soon thereafter.

Under the tutelage of rookie-coach Kerr, the Bulls went 33–48 in their first season and made the playoffs. Their record was the best ever for an NBA expansion franchise in its first season. Kerr was named the NBA Coach of the Year and Rodgers led the NBA in assists with 11.2 handouts per game. Rodgers and Sloan were named to the NBA All-Star Game.

But the Bulls barely made a blip on the Chicago sports scene, losing to the more popular, more established Blackhawks for wintertime sports interest.

16 Johnny "Red" Kerr

Michael Jordan and Derrick Rose are loved in Chicago for what they did for the Bulls on the court. But no person was more beloved in the Bulls organization than Johnny "Red" Kerr, the former coach, business manager, and broadcaster.

Kerr was a local high school hero from Tilden High School who went to the University of Illinois (reaching the NCAA Final Four in 1952), played pro ball for the Syracuse Nationals, Philadelphia 76ers, and Baltimore Bullets of the NBA, and as a starting rookie center led the Nationals to the league title in 1954–55. He played 12 years in the pros, most of them with Syracuse, was a three-time All-Star, and averaged 14 points and 11 rebounds.

In high school, he led Tilden to the Chicago Public League title in 1950. At the University of Illinois, Kerr led the Illini to the Final Four of the NCAA tournament in '52.

His true claim to fame as a professional basketball player was his so-called "iron-man" streak. He played 844 straight games (917 if you include playoff games) over his career, breaking the previous NBA record of 706 held by legendary big man Dolph Schayes. Kerr's streak remained intact until the early '80s.

As Kerr's career ended with the Baltimore Bullets, a Chicago man named Dick Klein was putting together a bid for a franchise in Chicago. When the team was finally announced and Klein was looking for a coach, he received numerous calls and letters suggesting he give Kerr a chance. Kerr's fame within Chicago basketball circles had only grown through his college and pro days, and his good nature seemed a perfect fit for an expansion franchise.

Klein wanted another Chicago legend, DePaul coach Ray Meyer, but Meyer, a college coach through and through, was not interested. That's when Klein turned to Kerr, who was still an active player with the Baltimore Bullets at the time.

Oddly, Kerr was actually selected by the Bulls as a player in the expansion draft, in a backroom deal Klein manufactured for financial reasons. As a rookie coach in 1966–67, Kerr led the Bulls to the playoffs in their first season (the first expansion team to reach the playoffs) and was named Coach of the Year. The Bulls again made the playoffs the following season under Kerr, who left the team in '68 to coach another expansion team, the Phoenix Suns.

Kerr eventually returned to the Bulls to serve as a business manager, but found his true calling off the court when he joined the Bulls broadcast team as a color commentator on TV and radio in 1975 at the suggestion of play-by-play man Jim Durham. Kerr remained on the Bulls' TV or radio broadcasts through the 2007–08 season.

For a short while, Kerr had a restaurant named after him near Chicago Stadium. His large personality and upbeat attitude proved significant as the Bulls struggled, then eventually grew into an NBA championship team.

Kerr died of prostate cancer on February 26, 2009, only a few hours after the death of fellow Bulls legend Norm Van Lier.

17 1992 World Champions

For the start of the 1991–92 NBA season, the Bulls made the rare roster move of not making any roster moves. Coming off of their first NBA championship, the Bulls maintained nearly the same 12-man roster from the season before, with the exception that outside shooting threat Bobby Hansen, a collegiate hero at nearby University of Iowa, was picked up from Sacramento for Dennis Hopson, to play the unenviable role of Michael Jordan's backup at shooting guard.

The difference in the '91–92 season was that the Bulls were no longer a surprise to anyone. That did not deter them from being the most dominant team in recent NBA history, winning 67 games, two shy of the league record for wins in a season. They took no one by surprise, and it didn't much matter.

The Bulls won 37 of their first 42 games and won 14 games straight from November 6 to December 6, a team record. They lost focus through January and February, dropping some games they probably should have won.

But the Bulls found their stride again and won 19 of their last 22 games to finish 67–15, their best record ever.

The Bulls swept the Miami Heat in the first round of the playoffs, and Jordan had 56 points in the dramatic Game 3 in Miami. The next round was against the New York Knicks and coach Pat Riley, who had developed a spirited rivalry with Bulls coach Phil Jackson.

The Knicks won Game 1 in Chicago, but the Bulls returned the favor in Game 3 in New York, and the series was even at 2–2 going into Game 5 of the best-of-seven series in Chicago. The Bulls won that game, but the Knicks won again in New York, setting up a decisive Game 7 at Chicago Stadium. The Bulls crushed the Knicks 110–81 in that game to advance to the Eastern Conference Finals.

The Bulls survived some difficulties against Cleveland in the Conference finals but won the series four games to two and ended up playing the Portland Trail Blazers in the finals.

In that decisive Game 6, the Bulls trailed by 17 points late in the third quarter, and coach Phil Jackson pulled most of his starters and played a lineup of Bobby Hansen, Stacey King, B.J. Armstrong, Scott Williams, and Scottie Pippen. Led by some hot shooting from Hansen, the Bulls came back into the game. The decision to go with the second string indicated the Bulls' strength of roster and solidified Jackson's stature as a genius coach.

Midway through the fourth quarter, Jackson reinserted Jordan and the other starters and the Bulls won the game and the title running away.

This time, however, the Bulls won at home. The trophy ceremony was held in the locker room at Chicago Stadium, but the

The Shrug

One thing people don't often remember about Michael Jordan from his early years is that he was not considered a really good outside shooter. He made himself into one eventually, but the first derogatory thing said about him as a pro was that he could not hit consistently from the outside.

In his first four NBA seasons, Jordan shot less than 20 percent from three-point range. By the 1990–91 season, he had improved that percentage to 31 percent, but was shooting just 27 percent from long range in the regular season of the '91–92 campaign.

In the '90 NBA All-Star Weekend Long Distance Shootout, Jordan had embarrassed himself with the lowest score ever achieved in the contest.

When the Bulls found themselves matched against Clyde Drexler and the Portland Trail Blazers in the '92 NBA Finals, Jordan was psyched to do it again, win another title, add to his legacy. But he did not know he would use the three-point shot to achieve his goal.

Jordan scored 35 points in *the first half* of Game 1 of the series, a record for one half in an NBA finals game. And in that half he made six three-point shots, another finals record. When he made the sixth of those shots, he jogged down to the defensive end of the court, turned to the national broadcast team sitting courtside, and offered a shrug. It was as if he was saying, "I don't know where that is coming from."

That's kind of what he said after the game as well, following the Bulls' dominating 122–89 win.

"I didn't know what I was doing," Jordan said. "I was in a zone. My threes felt like free throws."

Jordan eventually improved his career three-point shooting percentage to 32.7 percent, and in the '95–96 season, upon his return from retirement he shot a career best (for a full season) of 42.7 percent.

team decided to share the moment with the fans. They climbed the stairs from the locker room level to the floor level and ran out onto the basketball floor to the cheers of the happy throng. Michael Jordan jumped onto the scorer's table and waved a towel at the fans to incite them further.

Once again, Michael Jordan swept the MVP honors, winning for the regular season and the NBA Finals. He also made the NBA All-Defensive First Team and grabbed his sixth straight scoring title. Scottie Pippen made the NBA All-Defensive First Team as well.

The summer promised more basketball for the stars as Jordan and Pippen once again were named to the U.S. Olympic basketball team.

18 1993 World Champions

With great success comes great pressure and occasionally conflict. So it was for the Bulls as they prepared to chase a three-peat of championships.

Michael Jordan and Scottie Pippen came into camp exhausted after successfully winning the Olympic gold medal in basketball at the 1992 Summer Games in Barcelona, Spain. Two other starters, Bill Cartwright and John Paxson, were coming off summer knee surgery.

B.J. Armstrong replaced Paxson as the starting guard for the '92–93 season. He started 74 games that season, averaged 12.3 points per game and led the NBA in three-point shooting at 45.3 percent. Cartwright was still the starting center, but only played in 63 games while Will Perdue and Stacey King backed him up in the middle. Phil Jackson called off the dogs in some games, allowing the tired Bulls to have something left in the tank for the playoffs.

For the '92–93 season, the Bulls replaced Bobby Hansen with Trent Tucker to serve as Jordan's backup at shooting guard. The deep bench included veterans Rodney McCray and Darrell Walker, who happened to be a good friend of Jordan's.

The Bulls won 57 games that year and were far from the best team in the league. The Phoenix Suns won 62 games and the New York Knicks finished 60–22. The Houston Rockets and Seattle SuperSonics won 55 games and the Cleveland Cavaliers won 54. Everyone agreed the playoffs were going to be competitive.

But the Bulls cruised through the first two rounds of the playoffs, sweeping the Atlanta Hawks and the Cavaliers. That set up an Eastern Conference Final against coach Pat Riley and the New York Knicks.

In the two previous seasons, the Bulls had beaten the Knicks in the playoffs, once in the first round and then in the second round. Just as the Bulls needed years to approach the Detroit Pistons prior to the championships, the Knicks were trying to make a march on the Bulls.

For the '92–93 Eastern Conference Finals, the Knicks had home-court advantage and believed they were ready to take the next step.

The Knicks won the first two games at Madison Square Garden, and Jordan appeared human, going 22 for 59 in those games. The Knicks were using a bruising style of basketball, similar to the type of game the Pistons had used years earlier.

The Bulls won the next two games in Chicago, by 20 and 10 points, and Jordan had 29 points, 10 rebounds, and 14 assists to help steal Game 5 in New York, taking the lead in the series three games to two. The Bulls won the series at home in Game 6 to advance to the NBA Finals against Charles Barkley and the Phoenix Suns.

Again, the Bulls were without home-court advantage. But they reclaimed the edge by winning the first two games in Phoenix.

Game 3 in Chicago—the first of three games in a row at Chicago Stadium—went into triple overtime before the Suns won the game 129–121. The Bulls won Game 4 behind 55 points from Jordan, but the Suns avoided elimination by beating the Bulls in Game 5, forcing yet another trip to Phoenix.

Behind a newfound three-point threat from Jordan, Armstrong, Paxson, and Tucker, the Bulls led most of Game 6. But Phoenix opened a late lead in the fourth quarter and was up by four points with a minute and a half to go. Jordan scored to cut the lead to two, the Bulls forced the Suns into an air ball, and the Bulls had the ball again with 14 seconds left.

Jordan got the ball to Pippen, who went into the lane but had no clear shot. He threw the ball to Horace Grant on the left baseline, who sent the ball out to Paxson at the three-point arc, left of center. Paxson took the shot, using his straight-as-an-arrow jump, and hit the game-winning shot with three seconds left.

The Suns had one last chance to win. Veteran guard Kevin Johnson got the ball in the lane and took a 13-foot jumper, but Horace Grant blocked the shot and the game was over. The Bulls were three-time NBA champions.

No one knew that night that the championship streak would end, at least temporarily.

Jordan averaged 41 points during the finals. He won his seventh-straight scoring title, tying Wilt Chamberlain for most consecutive scoring titles. He once again was named NBA Finals MVP. Pippen joined Jordan on the All-Star team again, and was on the All-Defensive First Team.

19 The Years In Between

Bulls general manager Jerry Krause had big plans for the Bulls in the 1993–94 season.

He had finally convinced Croatian superstar Toni Kukoc to come to the United States. Kukoc was playing under a lucrative contract with a team in Italy at the time, and he had fought Krause's urgings for two years after being drafted by the Bulls in the 1990 draft.

But Kukoc finally felt he was ready and came to the United States in the summer of '93 with plans to play with Michael Jordan and Scottie Pippen, creating the greatest team in NBA history.

Krause had also signed Steve Kerr, the outside-shooting threat who seemed like a clone of former starter John Paxson; and another 14 feet of center in Canadian Bill Wennington and Australian Luc Longley. They were going to replace Bill Cartwright and Stacey King as part of the Bulls' three-headed monster.

Jordan's retirement left the Bulls without a starting shooting guard. Krause immediately signed former Bull Pete Myers, a journeyman talent with a similar size to Jordan.

From the championship teams, the Bulls still had Scottie Pippen, Horace Grant, B.J. Armstrong, Perdue, and Scott Williams. They managed to win 55 games in the '93–94 season and advanced to the Eastern Conference semifinals, again taking on the New York Knicks.

The series went seven games, and the Bulls were giving the Knicks all they could handle.

In Game 3 in Chicago, Pippen had his worst moment as a Bull. The Bulls trailed by one point with 1.8 seconds remaining, and Jackson called a timeout to design a play for Kukoc to take the final shot and Pippen to serve as a decoy. Pippen was so mad he refused to reenter the game.

Kukoc hit the game-winning shot, and Pippen became persona non grata among Bulls fans for years to come.

The Bulls won Game 4 and took the series to Game 7. The Bulls were leading the fifth game late when referee Hue Hollins called Pippen for a foul on New York's Hubert Davis. To many, the foul did not occur, and Hollins received a great deal of criticism for allowing Davis to go to the line to shoot the game-winning free throws.

Pippen had wanted to get the Bulls to the NBA Finals without Jordan leading the way, and he was denied by that call.

For the '94–95 season, Paxson and Cartwright were gone, as was Scott Williams and Horace Grant. Pippen was seeking a new deal from the Bulls and was getting nowhere. Bad blood existed all over the place.

Pippen, Kukoc, Armstrong, Kerr, and the three centers kept the team together for most of the year. Krause signed Jud Buechler and Ron Harper to help out, and the Bulls won 47 games, the least number of victories since the start of the championship run.

The '94–95 season was also the year the United Center opened, replacing Chicago Stadium, where the Bulls had won their titles. The United Center became known as "The House That Jordan Built" because it was a project started in response to the need to upgrade facilities for a championship team.

During that year, Michael Jordan made some unannounced visits to the team's practice facility to work out with the guys. Those visits preceded what seemed to be the inevitable return of Jordan to active participation. Jordan returned to the NBA on March 18, 1995.

With new life, the Bulls played the Charlotte Hornets in the first round of the playoffs and won three games to one. That set them up for a meeting with Shaquille O'Neal and the Orlando Magic.

Jordan was not in the best shape of his life. He struggled to do what he had always done, which was take over games, and the Magic won the semifinal series four games to two. Jordan's return was ended suddenly, but he developed a renewed desire to get back into top shape.

20 Jordan's Return

The Berto Center, the Bulls' practice facility in Deerfield, Illinois, is a slightly hidden, relatively small building. It has no signage that can be seen from either of its cross streets indicating its purpose.

Visitors must be buzzed into the building by team officials upstairs. To enter the inner sanctum, or to get to the team offices, one must get buzzed through a second door.

Players, coaches, and staff enter through a door that accesses the private parking lot in back.

The Berto Center is a good place to keep things secret if you want to do so.

In spring 1995, as Michael Jordan practiced with the Bulls in anticipation of his return from his first retirement, no one outside of the organization knew for sure what was going on. While there is a large plate-glass window between the Bulls' media room at the Berto Center and the practice floor inside, a large gray shade keeps unwanted eyes from viewing what goes on inside.

For more than a week, reports squeaked out from the Berto that Jordan was practicing with the Bulls in anticipation of his return. Details were impossible to come by; current members of the team said nothing.

The Bulls played home games against Cleveland and the Los Angeles Lakers, went to Washington for a game, then hosted Atlanta and Milwaukee between March 8 and March 18, when the rumors were at their strongest. Still, nothing was said about Jordan's upcoming decision.

Then, on March 18, in an era when announcements came via fax, machines around Chicago burned with the one-page, one-sentence, two-word announcement from Jordan's agent, David Falk. All it said was: "I'm back."

While it might have seemed a bit presumptive for Jordan and his people to assume everyone understood, the fact is everyone *did* understand. Jordan was ending his retirement, which included a remarkable effort to play professional baseball, and coming back to the game that put him at the pinnacle of athletic success, professional basketball.

On Sunday, March 19 in Indianapolis, Jordan took the floor with the Bulls for a game against the Indiana Pacers. The shock of seeing Jordan again in the familiar red uniform with "Bulls" on the front was followed by yet another shock.

Jordan's jersey, No. 23, had already been retired by the Bulls in a stirring, if premature, ceremony on November 1, 1994. So Jordan wore No. 45, the number he wore during his minor league baseball career and in junior high school. Jordan said he wanted to honor his father's memory by keeping No. 23 retired because his father had seen his last game in that jersey number.

New Jordan jerseys (No. 45) started finding their way into sporting goods stores as fans hurried to catch up with Jordan's decision.

In that first game, Jordan went seven for 28 from the field, and Jordan admitted he was a little embarrassed by how he played.

The first game for Jordan at the United Center was against Orlando on March 24. The electronic United Center sign at the corner of Madison and Wood on Chicago's west side had its own two-word announcement that night: "Michael's back."

Jordan's crowning achievement upon his return was at Madison Square Garden, and people who knew Jordan wondered if he had it planned all along. Jordan loved the bright lights, big-city atmosphere of the Garden, so it came as no surprise when he scored 55 points against the Knicks on March 28.

Making that game more special was that the winning basket was scored not on a basket by Jordan but on a dunk by center Bill Wennington, who received the perfect pass from Jordan to set up his thunder slam from the left side of the basket with just a few seconds remaining.

Jordan's return gave the Bulls a lift through the 1995 playoffs, but not enough to get them past the Orlando Magic in the second round of the postseason.

During the series, as his play seemed to suffer under the intensity of the playoffs, Jordan decided to go back to his No. 23 jersey in search of some of his former magic. It didn't work in '95, but Jordan remained in the No. 23 jersey for the rest of his Bulls career.

21 1997 World Champions

The summer after the 1996 title was a tumultuous one for the Bulls. Coach Phil Jackson, star guard Michael Jordan, and rebounding-fiend Dennis Rodman were all without contracts, and those deals had to be negotiated.

Meanwhile, Scottie Pippen and Toni Kukoc were playing in the World Championships for the U.S. and Croatia, respectively.

The entire '96–97 season was played in pain. Kukoc, Bill Wennington, and Luc Longley suffered basketball-related injuries, and Wennington's struggles with plantar fasciitis lasted into the playoffs that season.

For the '96–97 season, Bulls general manager Jerry Krause achieved a career-long dream. He added longtime Boston Celtics center Robert Parish, a favorite player of Krause's, to the roster to replace James Edwards as the third member of the center rotation

Rodman, Pippen, Jackson, and Jordan celebrate yet another NBA championship in Chicago's Grant Park.

("the three-headed monster"). Parish would serve as the No. 3 center behind Longley and Wennington, and ended up getting a great deal of playing time when the first two centers suffered injuries.

Despite the health issues, the Bulls still won 69 games, tying the Los Angeles Lakers for the second most wins in a season. It was the Lakers' record that the Bulls broke the previous season when they won 72 games.

The Bulls started the season winning their first 12 games. Then, after a loss at Utah, they won their next five. Add those numbers to the 72–10 record from the previous season and the Bulls went 89–11 over a 100-game span.

The Bulls lost two games in a row twice in '96–97. In December they lost at home against Miami and then on the road at Toronto. The last two games of the regular season were also losses, at Miami and at home against New York.

Jordan Picks a Team

When the Bulls won three straight NBA titles from 1991–93, they did so with virtually the same roster all three years. When they won three in a row from '96–98, they again used the same basic lineup for three years.

There were two players who were on all six Bulls championship teams, Michael Jordan and Scottie Pippen. Otherwise, the two roster groups were completely different from each other.

Two sets of teams, with two common elements, each won three titles in a row. So it's natural to want to compare the two teams and discuss which team would win a seven-game series against the other.

Jordan did it himself, once.

On a February night in Cleveland in '97, after the Bulls had won their first of three titles by setting an NBA record with 72 wins in the '95–96 season, Jordan agreed to compare the two lineups in a conversation with a beat reporter who had covered both sets of champions.

Keep in mind this conversation occurred before the Bulls won the second of three titles in the second three-peat. Still, the people involved were the same, and the concept still worked.

So Jordan looked at the '91–93 lineup of Jordan, Pippen, Bill Cartwright, Horace Grant, and John Paxson versus the '96 lineup of Jordan, Pippen, Luc Longley, Dennis Rodman, and Ron Harper.

Jordan gave the edge to Cartwright over Longley in the middle: "I think Bill had more because he was an aggressive player."

He gave a sort of edge to Paxson over Harper at the point guard position: "I'm not saying Paxson is better than Harper, but he fit into the system because he was around longer than Harper."

He gave the edge at power forward to Grant over Rodman, even though Rodman was in the midst of a streak of seven straight rebounding titles: "You could count on him every night. You know he is not going to go off the deep end. You don't have to contain him or his personality."

Next he rated the early Pippen against the later Pippen: "Scottie was more physically healthy in those days, but his confidence is strong here in this era. I think it is a standoff."

And how about Jordan versus Jordan? "I think it's a standoff, Michael Jordan vs. Michael Jordan," Michael Jordan said. "My knowledge of what I am capable of doing now overcomes some physical disabilities I have now."

In the first month of the season, after the Bulls lost their first game of the campaign at Utah, the team had a day off in Los Angeles. Jud Buechler, a native Californian and admitted surfer dude, took Longley, a native Australian, out body surfing. On a particularly active approach to land off a high wave, Longley rammed his shoulder into a hidden sand bar and suffered an injury that would keep him out until January.

Coach Phil Jackson, who openly believed his players needed to expand their horizons when the opportunity presented itself, handled the injury with aplomb, after blistering both Buechler and Longley in a private meeting for their bad decision to body surf.

In a game against the Lakers in December, Kukoc, Jordan, and Pippen all scored 30 points, marking the first time in team history such an event took place.

Rodman was suspended twice during the '96–97 season, first for a profanity-laced recorded complaint against the NBA and its officiating staff, and the second time for kicking a cameraman in the groin in Minneapolis after falling out of bounds chasing a loose ball.

During the All-Star festivities that year in Cleveland, the NBA decided to name the top 50 players in league history. While everyone expected Jordan to be on the list, it came as a complete surprise that the list also included Pippen.

At the All-Star Game itself, Jordan became the first player ever to record a triple-double with 14 points, 11 rebounds, and 11 assists.

The Bulls received locker-room visits that season from both President Bill Clinton (while in Washington to play the Bullets) and from First Lady Hillary Rodham Clinton (while in Chicago).

Once the Bulls got to the playoffs, they dispatched the upstart Bullets in three games and defeated the Atlanta Hawks in five. They found themselves again facing Alonzo Mourning and the Miami Heat for the Eastern Conference Finals but lost just once before heading to the NBA Finals against the Utah Jazz.

"I don't think anybody is going to win again until Michael retires," Miami coach Pat Riley said in response to the Bulls dismantling of his team.

Utah was making its first-ever appearance in the NBA Finals in '96. For years, their team had consisted of guard John Stockton and power forward Karl Malone and the others selected to surround them. They were also coached by Jerry Sloan, the Bulls' first hero and former coach, someone Phil Jackson greatly respected. Sloan's jersey, No. 4, was the first retired by the Bulls organization.

The Bulls won Game 1 on a basket by Jordan at the buzzer. The Bulls won the second game in easier fashion, then headed off to Salt Lake City for Games 3, 4, and maybe 5.

The Jazz won Game 3 by 11 points, with Malone scoring 37 points and grabbing 10 rebounds in the win. They also won Game 4, tying the series at two games apiece.

Years ago, during the '93 NBA Eastern Conference Finals against the New York Knicks, Michael Jordan was publicly criticized for spending an evening before a game gambling in Atlantic City. Years later, Dennis Rodman spent the night between Games 4 and 5 in Las Vegas without much of a whimper from the media.

In Game 5, Jordan played with a severe case of the flu. Even though he always sweated while he played, in that game he was drenched from the heat his body was giving off. But he scored 38 points on the way to a 90–88 win and command of the series with the final two games to be played in Chicago.

The Bulls won the series in Game 6, 90–86, thanks to a last-minute three-point shot by Steve Kerr, allowing him to enter the Bulls' history books in much the same way his three-point predecessor (and former Bulls assistant coach) John Paxson did a few years earlier.

For the fifth time in seven seasons, the Bulls were NBA champions.

22 Rose as MVP

In 2009, the Bulls were more than a decade removed from their last NBA championship. They knew they were never going to see another Michael Jordan, but they were not without hope that they would once again see a championship team someday.

By the 2009–10 NBA season, Bulls fans had come to realize they had a new special talent in Derrick Rose. His Rookie of the Year award solidified his standing with the community. Reports of his manic workout regimen in the summer reminded fans of the reports of Jordan's workout routine during his playing days. Fans were so excited to see what Rose was going to bring in his second NBA season.

Although the parallels to Jordan were obvious (Rookie of the Year from the guard position, ball-handling skills, strong moves to the basket), experts warned Bulls fans to be wary of making too many attempts at comparison. After all, Jordan was 6'6" and Rose was just 6'3". Jordan was Jordan, the greatest player to ever play the game. Rose was in his second season.

But just as Jordan injured himself in the fourth game of his second season and missed 64 games, Rose started his second season with a significant injury. He injured his ankle in the first preseason game and missed the rest of the preseason nursing the injury. Rose played from the start of the season but was clearly recuperating as the season went along.

Still, with the respect that comes from being Rookie of the Year, and the fact that the Bulls appeared to be making progress after their impressive playoff appearance from the year before, Rose was named as a reserve to the Eastern Conference All-Star team in his second season. He was the first Bulls player to play in the

Derrick Rose skies over LeBron James and the Miami Heat for a thunderous dunk in the 2011 playoffs. (Getty Images)

All-Star Game since 1998 when Jordan made his last appearance. Rose scored eight points with four assists in the game, played outdoors in Cowboys Stadium in Arlington, Texas.

Rose averaged 20.8 points in his second season and again led the Bulls to a 41–41 record and another playoff appearance in 2010. This time they were paired against the No. 1 seed Cleveland Cavaliers, led by LeBron James, and the Bulls lost the best-of-seven series in five games.

Rose received an accolade in the summer of 2010 when he was named to the U.S. Team for the 2010 FIBA Championships. The United States went unbeaten in the tournament, beating host Turkey for the title. Rose averaged 7.2 points for the team and earned another stripe in terms of basketball respect.

Before the summer started, Rose had promised he would come back with an improved three-point shot. When the 2010–11 preseason camp began, Rose appeared stronger and even more confident as a result of his international appearances.

When asked to make a prediction about how he would play in the upcoming season, Rose made an amazing proclamation:

"Why can't I be the MVP?"

He asked the question to the media the first day of workouts, and it seemed like a brazen statement. After all, the league still had LeBron James, Kobe Bryant, and Dwight Howard, to name a few. But Rose's words became a harbinger for the 2010–11 season.

During the season, Rose earned his first NBA All-Star starting nomination for the East squad. He continually raised his personal career highs, scoring 42 points against the San Antonio Spurs in February.

The Bulls, meanwhile, were slowly climbing up the league's ladder toward the best record. To the surprise of most observers, the Bulls ended up with a record of 62–20, best in the league, and Rose led the team with 25 points and 7.7 assists per game.

On May 1, 2011, Rose became the youngest player ever to be named Most Valuable Player. At the age of 22, he edged out former Baltimore Bullet Wes Unseld (23) as the youngest MVP ever. He joined Jordan as the only Bulls ever to be judged the Most Valuable Player for an NBA season.

Doug Collins

In 1986, the Bulls had a new regime. There was new owner Jerry Reinsdorf, new general manager Jerry Krause, and their new star,

Michael Jordan, who was healthy again after suffering from a broken foot the previous season.

The Bulls had fired Stan Albeck at the end of the '85 season and were looking for a coach who could work with Jordan to start a move toward a championship.

Krause, never afraid to take a chance, turned to Doug Collins, who was making a living as a CBS broadcaster after an injury-shortened professional career.

Collins was best known in Chicago for his time at Illinois State University, where he was a player and a starter on the 1972 U.S. Olympic basketball team. That was the team which was cheated out of a gold medal by the referees in the championship game against the Russians.

Krause was belittled for hiring a guy with no coaching experience who was only 35 years old. What they got was a man with a burning passion to teach the game of basketball and win.

"I was the kind of guy to roll up my sleeves and make something happen," Collins said.

His first team, the '86–87 Bulls, featured Jordan, Charles Oakley, longtime Bulls center Dave Corzine, and a bunch of players with reputations from college but little professional luster. The only guys who would stick around were first-round draft pick Brad Sellers (Jordan had wanted Johnny Dawkins from Duke and made no secret about it) and John Paxson, a guard picked up from San Antonio.

Almost as important as the roster was Collins' coaching staff, which included Tex Winter, a longtime pro and college coach whom general manager Jerry Krause loved, and Johnny Bach, a former college coach who had worked with Collins on the Olympic team.

In Collins' first year, the Bulls went 40–42. They made the playoffs but were swept by the Boston Celtics. However, Collins had already developed a reputation as a high-energy, high-intensity coach. He was always moving, rarely sat, and took losses hard.

Collins Was Meant To Be a Bull

During the summer of 1973, the Bulls arranged to trade guard Bob Weiss and center Clifford Ray to the Philadelphia 76ers for Doug Collins, who was the No. 1 pick of the '73 collegiate draft out of Illinois State University. But Ray did not pass the physical in Philadelphia and the deal was squashed.

Thirteen years later, in 1986, Collins became the head coach of the Bulls, and more than 20 years after that, he almost became coach of the Bulls a second time before they settled on Vinny Del Negro.

After Krause selected Scottie Pippen and Horace Grant in the '87 draft, Collins had a better team to work with. They went 50–32 (their first 50-win season since '73–74) and the Bulls advanced to the second round of the playoffs, beating the Cleveland Cavaliers 3–2 in the first round before falling in the Eastern Conference semifinal round to the Detroit Pistons 4–1.

During the '87–88 season, Collins and Jordan had a rough patch directly related to the competitive nature of both men.

When the Bulls scrimmaged, Jordan's team always won. Collins wanted scrimmages to be more competitive, so one day he allegedly changed the score of a scrimmage to test Jordan and to keep the game challenging. Jordan accused Collins of changing the score, stormed out of practice, and the relationship changed from that day forward.

The '87–88 season was also when the Bulls hired Phil Jackson to join Winter and Bach on Collins' staff. Again, it was a standard Krause reach, selecting a coach who was a proven winner in the CBA but had an out-of-the-box way of looking at basketball and life.

Collins' third year as coach was the first for Bill Cartwright, traded to the Bulls by the Knicks for Charles Oakley. Collins moved Pippen into the starting lineup ahead of Sellers, and the Bulls won 47 games.

The Bulls took the next step in the playoff progression by winning two series; the first against Cleveland (with Michael Jordan hitting "The Shot" to help the team advance) and the second against the New York Knicks and Oakley. They advanced to the conference finals, where they were again defeated by the Detroit Pistons.

Collins was now the Bulls' second-winningest coach of all time.

Unfortunately, Collins was also done as coach of the Bulls. Collins and Krause had clashed, and Reinsdorf, who regarded Collins very highly, felt Collins' high-strung personality was not the best for a team with its sights on a championship. "I knew it was the right decision for Doug," Reinsdorf said. "I really like him as a person, but he is driven, maybe to the detriment of his own benefit. I wanted to remove him from a situation where I thought he was going to grind himself up."

Reinsdorf later said, in one of his most famous quotes, that Collins brought the Bulls from Point A to Point B but was not the man to take them to Point C.

Reinsdorf, however, considered re-hiring Collins twice thereafter, when the Bulls were looking for a new coach in the 2000s. But Reinsdorf said he did not want to put a strain on the friendship he had with Collins, knowing that he might just have to fire him again someday.

24 Jordan at All-Star Games

Michael Jordan was invited to play in the NBA All-Star Game 14 times, which is basically every chance he could over his start-stop-start-stop career.

Jordan was always the All-Stars' All-Star. Every time he put on the All-Star uniform, he did so with the plan to be the best player on the floor. Although his playing time was determined by the coaching staff, he made the most of his appearances and was the NBA All-Star MVP three times in his career.

He was not the MVP of his first All-Star Game, even though he was the most talked-about player.

By the time the 1985 All-Star Game in Indianapolis rolled around, Jordan was already the talk of the league. His high-flying acrobatic playing style was not yet transferring to victories, but he was suddenly the most famous player in the league, and apparently some veterans took offense to that.

Reportedly led by Isiah Thomas, the MVP of the previous year's All-Star Game, some veterans conducted a "freeze-out" of Jordan, refusing to pass him the ball, thus making it impossible for him to show off.

Jordan was elected to the next year's game in Dallas but did not play because of a foot injury that kept him out of most of the season. By the 1987 game in Seattle, Jordan was ready to show his stuff again.

Then came the 1988 All-Star Game in Chicago. Even the fact that the city of Chicago got the All-Star Game for the first time since 1973 was a testament to Jordan's popularity.

The entire weekend turned out to be a coronation of sorts, from his controversial victory in the Slam Dunk Contest to his selection as the game's MVP. He scored 40 points, the most he ever scored in an All-Star Game, making 17 of 23 shots, with six free throws and eight rebounds in 29 minutes. Oddly, as the game wound down and the outcome was undetermined (even though the outcome of the All-Star Game rarely mattered) it was veterans Isiah Thomas and Larry Bird who were getting the ball to Jordan. The Bulls star, playing before a crowd that did not contain its appreciation, scored 16 points over the last six minutes. He finished two points shy of the record for an All-Star Game individual performance.

Jordan played in the next five All-Star games, averaging 24 points, before retiring in 1993.

Jordan returned to the NBA in the spring of 1995, then earned his 10th trip to the All-Star Game in 1996 in San Antonio's Alamodome. He wanted to let the world know he was truly back. He scored 20 points in 22 minutes, making eight of 11 shots and all four free throws he attempted. For that he earned his second MVP award.

The next year, in Cleveland's new downtown arena, Jordan accomplished something never before done in an All-Star Game. He scored only 14 points, but he also had 11 rebounds and 11 assists, creating the first-ever triple-double in All-Star Game history. Remarkably, he was not selected MVP that year. Instead it went to Glen Rice of the Charlotte Hornets, who scored 20 points in the third quarter of the game, setting a record for most points by a player in a single quarter.

Denied his third All-Star MVP award in 1997, Jordan came back in 1998 in New York's Madison Square Garden and put on another show. Jordan loved playing in the Garden in front of a crowd that knew a good show when it saw one. Jordan scored 23 points, with six rebounds, eight assists, and three steals to earn his third MVP.

The Bulls dynasty ended after the 1998 season. Phil Jackson, Jordan, and Scottie Pippen went their separate ways. Jordan "retired," only to come back after the new collective bargaining agreement was reached to play in 2001–02 and '02–03 for the Washington Wizards, with whom he had an owner's portion. He played in the All-Star Game in both '02 and '03 and scored 20 points in his last appearance, making only nine of 27 shots. For the 2003 game, Vince Carter gave up his starting spot so that Jordan could start for the Eastern Conference club.

By playing in the All-Star Game as a Wizard, Jordan became the all-time leading scorer in All-Star Game history, passing Kareem Abdul-Jabbar.

Jordan in Slam Dunk Contests

Michael Jordan did not invent the slam dunk.

There were dunk artists who came before Jordan. Chief among them was Julius Erving, known as Dr. J., who started his career in the ABA before coming to the NBA. Dominique Wilkins, the Human Highlight Film, preceded Jordan as well, and his athletic dunking style was certainly a precursor to what Jordan did.

But Jordan brought a strength and artistry to the scoring technique. It was a part of his game when he came to the NBA, and he perfected it for use during the NBA's slam dunk competitions in the All-Star weekend festivities.

The slam dunk was first allowed in the NCAA in 1976, which was the same year the ABA held its first slam dunk contest. The NBA incorporated it in the 1983–84 season, the year before Jordan came to the league.

Larry Nance of Cleveland won the initial contest in '84, and Wilkins won in '85, which was the first year Jordan participated. Wilkins and Jordan ended up in the finals of that competition, and Wilkins won with two perfect scores.

Jordan was already a showman. He took a piece of white athletic tape and put it on the floor at the free throw line to indicate where he was going to jump from. With a pair of necklaces dangling from around his neck (an affectation he soon eliminated), and

Jordan throws down a perfect dunk during the 1988 contest.

with his tongue fully extended from his mouth, Jordan duplicated the dunk first seen from Erving almost a decade before.

The contest ended with Jordan making a cradle dunk, while Wilkins offered a dunk in which he jumped, brought the ball down to between his knees, then brought it up and into the net. Wilkins was awarded the victory, but a duel of dunking had been created that night.

In 1986, Jordan was injured, and Wilkins' diminutive Atlanta teammate Spud Webb (5'7") won the contest.

In 1987, Jordan won the contest in Seattle. Wilkins was injured and unable to participate.

So the first rematch of the 1985 competition occurred three years later at Chicago Stadium, home of the Bulls. To this day it is considered the most epic of All-Star Slam Dunk moments from a competitive standpoint.

Jordan and Wilkins ended up in the finals of the competition. Wilkins went first with his final dunk and threw the ball high off the backboard above the rim, then jumped, caught the ball, and slammed it home for a dramatic dunk that gave him 145 points in three attempts. Jordan had 97 and needed a good score to beat Wilkins.

Jordan did it again, taking off from just inside the free throw line. Holding the ball in one hand, he brought the ball down and then up again for the dunk that earned him a perfect 50-point score and the title.

Many people believed Wilkins' dunks were superior to Jordan's, although Jordan had the signature leap from the free throw line to a thunder dunk. The photograph of Jordan rising in the air to complete the dunk, with the fans and others behind him in the stands, is one of the most iconic photographs ever taken of Jordan.

The dunks were voted on by a panel of judges, but it would have been hard for the judges to ignore the cheers of the home crowd after Jordan's dunks. Wilkins may have gotten jobbed, but the Slam Dunk is a popularity contest and a fan event, and the final score was not a surprise.

Jordan retired from the event after the 1988 contest. Because the NBA wanted Jordan to continue to participate in the weekend events, he once agreed to participate in the Long Distance Shootout, a three-point shooting contest, but he finished with the worst score in the event's history and only did that once.

In 1990, Scottie Pippen participated in the contest but did not win.

26 Jordan's Injury

Heading into the 1985–86 season, Jordan had raised the anticipation level of fans everywhere with his first-year performance. The Bulls made draft-day deals that allowed them to pick up forward Charles Oakley, who'd terrorized opponents on the boards playing for small school Virginia Union.

At the end of the '84–85 season, the Bulls released Rod Thorn as general manager and named Jerry Krause VP of basketball operations. They also changed head coaches, removing Kevin Loughery and installing veteran NBA coach Stan Albeck.

The day before the '85–86 season began, the Bulls traded forward David Greenwood to San Antonio for veteran guard George "The Iceman" Gervin, one of the most prolific scorers in NBA history, who was at the end of his long career.

The Bulls won their first three games that season, but in the third game—their first road game, at Golden State—Jordan broke his foot. He missed the next 64 games and the Bulls' season appeared to be over. The Bulls lost eight of their first nine after the injury and never managed to win more than three games in a row.

Orlando Woolridge, a Notre Dame product who had been with the team before Jordan's arrival, led the team in scoring 26 times before he got injured as well. The Iceman led the team in scoring 18 times, but the Bulls were scrambling offensively, waiting for Jordan's return.

Jordan offended the Bulls by deciding to return home to North Carolina for his rehabilitation. The team wanted him close to his new home to keep an eye on their investment. The disagreement became the first controversy of Jordan's professional career.

The Bulls front office was extremely cautious about Jordan's return, not wanting to bring him back until they had assurances from doctors that he was 100 percent healthy. Jordan, however, wanted desperately to get back into the game, and bad blood ensued between Jordan and new general manager Jerry Krause.

Jordan was activated on March 14, but he was not allowed to play a full game. With coach Albeck obeying Krause's time restraints, Jordan was placed on a playing-time limit for the first 10 games. The Bulls lost six of the first seven games upon Jordan's return.

In one game, Albeck pulled Jordan from a very close game with 30 seconds remaining because Jordan had reached his time limit. It was a move of defiance in the face of the team's restrictive measures, and it cost Albeck his job at the end of the season.

When Jordan was allowed to play a full game, going against New York on March 29, he scored 24 points and led the Bulls to victory. The Bulls won six of their last 10 games to get into the playoffs with a record of 30–52, which is a horrible record to have going into the playoffs, but it turned out to be noteworthy anyway.

He came back with 15 games left and terrorized the league, and then went on to score an all-time high (still) 63 points in the playoffs, but they did lose in the first round to Boston.

Through the rest of his career with the Bulls, not including 1995, when he came back from his first retirement in March of that season, Jordan never played less than 78 games in a season. In 12 full seasons with the Bulls, Jordan played all 82 games eight times.

27 Jordan Scores 63

During the 1985–86 season, Michael Jordan missed 64 games with a broken foot. It was his second season in the league, it was his first significant career injury, and he caused a big stir within the team, wanting to come back earlier than doctors recommended. Then, when he did return to active duty, he wanted to play more minutes than the doctors allowed.

He returned in March of that year, and although he was initially limited in playing time, he played 15 games and somehow got the Bulls into the playoffs with a record of 30–52.

In the first round, the Bulls were set to play the Boston Celtics, who were still on their legendary march to championships behind Larry Bird, Kevin McHale, Dennis Johnson, and Robert Parish. The Celtics won 67 games in 1985–86, just two shy of tying the league record of 69. The Bulls were going to be no match for the mighty Celtics in the five-game series.

And they weren't. The best-of-five series was over in the minimum three games. But Jordan—whose highest point total of the shortened season was 33 in the second game of the regular season—was ready for the task.

The first game of the series was held at Boston Garden, and even though Jordan scored 49 points, the Bulls lost 123–104. Jordan had proven he was healthy again, and NBA veterans were already shaking their heads at the scoring ability of this second-year pro.

Then came Game 2. Jordan scored 17 points in the first quarter, but just six in the second, giving him 23 points at halftime. In the third quarter, Jordan scored 13 more before adding 18 in the fourth quarter as he tried to pull the Bulls to victory in a close game. Jordan's last two points of regulation were free throws that sent the game into overtime. He'd been fouled on a missed three-point shot, which presently provides for three free throw attempts, but in 1986 the rule only called for two, and the game was going into overtime. Jordan had 54 points in regulation.

The Bulls could have won the game in the first extra period if Jordan had been able to add to his five points in those five extra minutes with a last-second 15-foot jumper, which he missed. Jordan scored four points in the second overtime as Boston took over and won 135–131.

Playing in 53 of the possible 58 minutes of the game, Jordan made 22 of 41 shots, 19 of 21 free throws, had five rebounds, six assists, and one new fan in Larry Bird.

"That was God disguised as Michael Jordan," Bird said. "I couldn't believe anybody could do that against the Boston Celtics."

It was the most points ever scored against the Celtics in a playoff game.

Jordan scored only 19 points in Game 3 when the series moved to Chicago. The Celtics had swept the series, but Jordan had swept the nation off its collective feet.

28 Attend a Game at the United Center

Among professional sports, basketball probably translates to television better than most others. The floor is easy to capture, the ball is easy to see, and the action is back and forth in a patterned manner.

But like most other professional sports, seeing it on TV is nothing like seeing it live.

The United Center is one of the most attractive basketball arenas in the country, and for a Bulls game it is a lively place full of non-stop action. Even a trip to the bathroom is an invitation to peruse the many concourse displays the Bulls present.

Sometimes, for special occasions, the Bulls pull out the six NBA championship trophies and put them in a display case opposite the concourse entrance to their merchandise shop, Fandemonium.

On the 100 and 300 concourses, the Bulls always have a couple of live bands performing music. Sometimes they are playing classics from the 1940s, sometimes they go for Motown from the 1960s, sometimes they play show tunes, and sometimes they get bands who can play more contemporary tunes. There is always room for a little dancing as well.

Food and drink are everywhere.

Once you enter the arena area, your senses are bombarded by sound, lights, and action. From above, the electronic scoreboard and monitors keep up a constant stream of information and videos. On the floor, from the time the gates open, two teams are warming up, the Luvabulls are practicing dance routines, or Benny the Bull is tooling around in some contraption or another to entertain the early-arriving crowd.

For your first visit, it is imperative that you get into your seats 15 minutes before the announced game start time. That's when the video board becomes the focus of attention.

For about two minutes, the Bulls present a video tribute to everything great that has ever happened to the franchise. There are video clips of Johnny "Red" Kerr and Jerry Sloan from the first years of the franchise, Bob Love and Chet Walker from the first real heyday of the team, then a fast forward to the players from the first three-peat: Michael Jordan, Scottie Pippen, Bill Cartwright, Horace Grant, and John Paxson. A few more clips of Jordan then are followed by a tribute to the second three-peat team: Jordan, Pippen, Dennis Rodman, Luc Longley, Ron Harper, and Steve Kerr. Finally, they show clips of the current team, which in 2011–12 included Derrick Rose, Joakim Noah, and Luol Deng.

After the history lesson comes the attack of the Bulls. The video begins with a depiction of the city of Chicago, which is then interrupted by the sound of thundering hooves as a bevy of digitally created Bulls charge through the city streets toward the United Center. There, outside one of the stadium gates, the Bulls blast through the team bus for the visiting team, and that signals that it is time for the team introductions.

Once the game begins, the fun is constant. Every timeout is occupied, either by video games or performances on the floor. There are races, dance performances, Benny skits, and things falling from the rafters.

For some people, the highlight of the game, other than a Bulls victory, is the donut race, when characters from the donut chain Dunkin' Donuts race on a video clip. Fans are given a numbered card, and if their numbered donut wins the race, they get free donuts or coffee the next day.

Still, all the sideshow is just a momentary distraction from the excitement of a live NBA game. Nothing compares to that moment in a game when the Bulls take control, dominate on either the offensive or defensive end, and prepare to claim another victory.

The Triangle

During the championship years, the Bulls had many components that made them a title-contending team. They had the talents of Michael Jordan and Scottie Pippen on both ends of the floor, and the coaching talents of Phil Jackson on the sideline.

One aspect of the dynasty that gets mentioned but rarely held to the same bright light as the people involved was the Triangle Offense (also known as the triple-post offense). Many will tell you the Bulls succeeded offensively because of their devotion to the special design of the offense.

The triple-post offense (it was also called the Triangle because that made it easier to understand) was designed in the 1940s by Sam Barry, who coached for the University of Southern California and was elected into the Basketball Hall of Fame in 1978. One of Barry's players at USC was Tex Winter, who grew up to be the basketball coach at Kansas State, among other places, and refined the Triangle Offense to a more modern game.

The tenets of the Triangle seem rather simple. A center sets up in the low post, becoming the fulcrum of a swinging triangle between himself, a guard, and a forward. The other guard sets up at the top of the key and the other forward is at the high post as a release or swing point for the strong side offensive patterns.

According to Winter, the offense is always effective because it has options no matter how the defense plays it.

The key to the offense is knowing where your teammates are going to be in all situations, knowing your options will be there when pressed one way or another. It takes timing, it takes practice, and it takes a strong belief in your teammates, knowing they will be where they are supposed to be.

Michael Jordan hated it.

The Triangle Offense does not prohibit strong individual moves to the basket, but it breaks down when such individual moves occur. Jordan was the king of breaking down defenses by himself, finding open spaces to move to, using his speed to get past a line of defense or his breakneck stops to get a defense moving in the wrong direction for an open short jumper.

The Triangle Offense is not a solo gig. It is a dance, a precise movement of pieces to achieve a goal. Penetration in the Triangle comes by way of passing the ball, not passing the defender.

Bulls general manager Jerry Krause fell in love with Winter during his years as a scout because Winter loved to talk basketball, as did Krause. Both men were single-minded. Winter preached the triple-post offense to Krause, and when Krause had the opportunity to hire Winter as an assistant coach to Stan Albeck in 1985, he strongly suggested the team look into using the Triangle Offense.

When Phil Jackson was elevated to head coach for the '89–90 season after Doug Collins was fired, Jackson bought into the Triangle. The movement of the offense, and the fact that the players outside of the post are considered interchangeable, worked with his philosophical training.

When the Detroit Pistons used the Jordan Rules to isolate its defense on Jordan, the Triangle saved the day. No one player in the Triangle is more important than another, and if a defense is going to concentrate on one player with two of its own, the Triangle is played with an extra man. Since spacing is so important to the Triangle (all players must maintain 10 to 15 feet from each other to have the proper spacing), a one-man advantage became huge.

Jackson maintained use of the Triangle when he took his coaching chops to the Los Angeles Lakers. Kobe Bryant won his five NBA titles using the Triangle for Jackson, who taught the offense to assistant Kurt Rambis, who in turn used it in his first head coaching job in Minnesota.

In 2011, Tex Winter was inducted into the Basketball Hall of Fame for his work as a college coach and his development of the Triangle Offense.

30 Phil Jackson, Philosopher

There was always something different about Phil Jackson.

The first time he interviewed for a job with the Bulls, he showed up dressed as if he had just come off the beach, which he apparently had. He was wearing a straw hat, among other things, and his devil-may-care attitude cost him his first opportunity in the NBA.

Although he straightened up enough to get a job that eventually grew into one of the great basketball coaching careers of all time, Jackson remained a counter-culture visionary. The standard rules of basketball, both on the court and off, did not mesh with Jackson's life journey.

Jackson grew up in a strict religious upbringing in Montana. Both of his parents were preachers. The family lived in a very remote area, and Jackson had limited social experiences growing up. Growing up in the 1950s and '60s, there were still Native American influences in Montana, and Jackson became exposed to them.

After a stellar college career at the University of North Dakota, Jackson was drafted by the New York Knicks in '67, a time of great social upheaval in America. Jackson became exposed to the counter culture first in college and then in New York, and it formed the man he was to become.

In college, Jackson began a serious study of mysticism, which eventually led him to read *Zen and the Art of Motorcycle Maintenance*, once considered the most accessible read on Zen philosophy. Jackson, who had cast aside his religious upbringing from childhood as too restrictive, was opening up.

In 1975, Jackson published his first book, a telling of his life in the NBA that included discussion of his drug use. It was believed that book kept him from receiving NBA job offers for many years, even though he had spent two years as an assistant coach in New Jersey.

After several successful years coaching in the old Continental Basketball Association, a minor league for pro players, Jackson got his chance with the Bulls. After two years as an assistant, he was allowed to become head coach, and the rest is history.

Stories of his coaching philosophies abound. His office at the Bulls' practice facility, the Berto Center, was filled with Native American artifacts, and he often used Native American philosophies in his coaching. He used a tom-tom to signal team meetings. He would burn incense in the locker room to ward off difficult spirits.

One day, during the second three-peat, Jackson hired a yoga expert to teach the Bulls the art of relaxation. Like with most of Jackson's ideas, this one was met with slight scorn and ridicule, but the players did it. Everything else Jackson had done seemed to work, so they gave that a try.

Jackson would often splice scenes from popular movies into the team's game films, and very often the point of the movie scenes was lost on the team. They would leave the sessions and discuss the movie choices, trying to glean the meaning Jackson was offering.

The Bulls took two long road trips every year, one in November when the circus occupied Chicago Stadium or the United Center, and one in late January and early February, when an ice show took over. Jackson would always give the players books he had specifically chosen for that player and suggest they read it during the trip. Usually, the players complied, although they again found the entire process unusual.

Jackson's most noticeable in-game philosophy was to allow the players to work their way out of jams. Time and again, over the years, when it appeared the Bulls needed a timeout to get their collective act together, Jackson would sit and wait, watching to see if the team could gather itself by itself. This philosophy worked well when the Bulls got into tighter playoff games and timeouts were precious.

In 1995, between the first three-peat and the second three-peat, Jackson penned a book titled *Sacred Hoops, Spiritual Lessons of a Hardwood Warrior* in which he discussed his ability to be himself in the world of professional basketball. In the introduction he writes: "This is a book about a vision and a dream. When I was named head coach of the Chicago Bulls in 1989, my dream was not just to win championships, but to do it in a way that wove together my two greatest passions: basketball and spiritual exploration."

Chapter titles included: "If You Meet Buddha in the Lane, Feed Him the Ball," and "Being Aware is More Important than Being Smart." Such philosophies drove Jackson through his coaching career.

In 2001, Jackson and his close friend Charley Rosen wrote a book together titled *More than a Game.* It again reflected Jackson's interest in things beyond the game of basketball that can be used to influence the game of basketball.

Be Like Mike

One of the most popular advertising campaigns in which Michael Jordan promoted Gatorade had children singing "I wanna be like Mike." "Be Like Mike" became the tag line that was repeated over and over again when Jordan's name came up.

For Gatorade, to be like Mike meant drinking their product. For kids, to be like Mike meant to hit the game-winning shot from the top of the free throw line.

Jordan actually accomplished that feat twice, and both times in memorable situations. He had The Shot against the Cleveland Cavaliers in the 1989 playoffs, when he drained the winner over guard Craig Ehlo, landed on his feet, and triple-pumped his fist as teammate Brad Sellers gathered him up in his arms to begin the celebration.

The second shot occurred in Jordan's last game as a Bull, when he pushed Utah's Bryon Russell out of the way and hit a jumper from above the free throw line, then stood frozen with his shooting hand extended as the ball went into the hoop and the Bulls won the 1998 NBA title.

In either case, thousands of kids found themselves on basketball courts practicing their last-second attempts, counting the time down themselves, producing pressure where none existed, re-creating the situation Jordan was in, pretending their shot was going to win an important game, or a title, just as Jordan's did.

There are other ways to pretend to be Michael Jordan. One of them requires extreme concentration. Try dribbling hard to the basket, ball coming off your right hand, with your tongue hanging out of your mouth like a thirsty St. Bernard. This may take some practice. You may need to get a tongue extension. And please try to avoid biting yourself on the tongue after you land from your jump shot.

Perhaps you want to impersonate Scottie Pippen. The easiest way to do that is to practice your bank shots. Nobody in the NBA could hit a 15- to 18-foot shot off the glass the way Pippen could. The other Pippen asset you could try to impersonate was his defense, but you are going to need another player to accomplish that task.

More than one Bulls fan has tried to impersonate Bill Cartwright's free throw style. It's kind of like a corkscrew, starting with the ball waist high, bringing it up in a semicircle to your face before letting go of the shot. Don't worry if you can't make that shot; it's going to take a lot of practice, and you will never look good doing it. Cartwright certainly never looked good doing it.

Newer Bulls fans can begin to practice their impersonation of MVP Derrick Rose. You are going to need some speed to pull this off, but dribble through some cones (or people who are willing to stand still), cradle the ball in your right hand as you jump toward the hoop, then put the ball high off the glass, almost to the top of the backboard, and watch it fall through the hoop for another amazing two-pointer.

Another fun Bulls-related exercise requires a lot of basketballs and probably a helper or two. You can pretend to be Craig Hodges competing in the All-Star three-point contest, which he won twice. He once hit 19 consecutive shots in a single round of 25 shots, five each from five different spots on the floor. This game probably requires at least six basketballs and a very fast assistant chasing down the balls and getting them to the next spot on the floor. But give it a try.

Tom Thibodeau

John Paxson's first coaching hire sure seemed like a good one. In 2003, he hired former Michigan State and NBA guard Scott Skiles, who had already had success coaching the Phoenix Suns, as his coach for the Bulls.

Skiles was a no-nonsense coach. He demanded strong play and brooked no lack of effort. He was the hard-nosed, driven coach Paxson wanted for his young team.

But Skiles could not last. His style had always seemed a bit abrasive, and eventually he and Paxson realized the team was no longer responding to his coaching demands. A change was made, although Paxson was disappointed that it was necessary.

After allowing Skiles' assistant Jim Boylan to coach, Paxson had to go find a permanent replacement. His first stop was to former Phoenix coach Mike D'Antoni, a known offensive-minded coach who was also being wooed by the New York Knicks. New York won that contest, in part because Bulls owner Jerry Reinsdorf was not sold on the no-defense game plan D'Antoni imparted.

Next on the list was former Bulls coach Doug Collins, who had been dragged back into coaching by Michael Jordan when Jordan was looking for someone to help his Washington Wizards get into the postseason. Collins, considered one of the best teaching coaches of his time, was a very popular choice for the Bulls position. However, Reinsdorf decided it was a bad idea because he and Collins were so close from Collins' previous time as Bulls coach in the 1980s, and he did not want to ever have to be in the position of once again firing his good friend, as he did in '89.

Those two decisions put Paxson behind the eight ball. He needed a coach, and he settled for Vinny Del Negro, a former NBA guard who had decided he wanted to become an NBA coach even though he had no bench experience.

Del Negro proved to be a mistake. His lack of coaching knowledge was regularly evident. He often had rookie Derrick Rose on the bench late in games, when his talents would have seemed most useful. His coaching-strategy sessions in game huddles appeared muddled, and he often turned to more experienced assistant coaches to produce ideas.

In two seasons under Del Negro, the Bulls went 41–41 twice. But the experiment was considered a failure, so Paxson went searching again. This time, it appeared he got it right.

After eight years coaching at the college level, Tom Thibodeau became an NBA assistant coach in 1989. He spent the next 22 years as an NBA assistant, working for Minnesota, Seattle, San Antonio, Philadelphia, New York, Houston, and Boston. Along the way, he developed a strong reputation for his defensive-coaching philosophies. While with the New York Knicks, the team set an NBA record by holding 33 consecutive opponents under 100 points.

While with the Boston Celtics, he helped the team become the best defensive club in the NBA, and along the way they won the 2008 NBA title with him as associate head coach.

The Bulls finally gave him the head coaching job he had sought, and he earned his salary in his first year. The Bulls became the league's best defensive team, using a help defense and his club's remarkable athleticism to stop the high-flying NBA talent. For his efforts, and the team's remarkable run to the best record in the league in 2010–11, Thibodeau was named NBA Coach of the Year, one of the first rookie head coaches ever to receive that award.

33 Phil Jackson's Assistant Coaches

Phil Jackson was an important assistant coach for the Bulls when he sat beside Doug Collins. But then Collins was fired, and Jackson became head coach. He peopled his bench with old-school basketball knowledge, and as the Bulls went on to win six titles in eight years, those assistants would become legendary themselves.

Tex Winter, Johnny Bach, and Jim Cleamons were instrumental in the success of the Bulls through the first three championship seasons, from 1991–93. They each had their job to do, they each did it in their own special way, and they each contributed to the dynasty that is the Chicago Bulls of the 1990s.

Winter's influence is well-known and an integral part of NBA lore. Winter designed the triple-post offense (also known as the Triangle Offense), an elegant offensive scheme that he used as a college coach (at Marquette, Kansas State, Washington, Northwestern, and Long Beach State) and as a pro head coach in Houston before bringing it to the Bulls.

Tex Winter was a pet project for Bulls general manager Jerry Krause, who loved Winter's mind for basketball and his ability to make it all sound so simple. When Krause hired Jackson to become head coach after firing Collins, he indicated he wanted Jackson to use Winter's triple-post with the Bulls.

Jackson liked the Triangle because it was precise and used all of the talents of all of the players. It was like the motion offense he had used while with the New York Knicks as a player.

Johnny Bach was a former college coach at Fordham and Penn State. He had been an NBA head coach at Golden State. He was known for his hard-nosed defensive coaching, and he started his career with the Bulls because of his relationship with Doug Collins, whom Bach had coached in the Olympics in 1972.

When the Bulls acquired Horace Grant and Scottie Pippen in 1987, Bach found the tools he needed to devise a strong defense. He called the two kids "The Dobermans" for their endless pursuit of the ball.

Bach and Winter were each in their late sixties when they joined the Bulls, but they could not have been less alike otherwise. Bach was a former military man, ramrod straight and strident in everything he did. Winter seemed professorial and grandfatherly, and seemed more country to Bach's city.

Cleamons was more Jackson's contemporary in age. They had been teammates during their professional careers. Cleamons was a liaison for players, someone they could talk to because he was closer in age and not quite as set in his ways. Cleamons remained with Jackson in Los Angeles.

Bach retired after the 1994 season in a clash with Krause, and he was replaced by longtime NBA coach Jimmy Rodgers, who served with Jackson from 1994 through the second three-peat that ended in 1998. In 1996, Cleamons left for a head-coaching job with the Dallas Mavericks and Frank Hamblen joined the coaching roster.

Winter and Hamblen stayed with the team through the first post-dynasty year with Tim Floyd as coach. Both later joined Jackson when he began coaching the Los Angeles Lakers.

34 Jordan Retires

In late July 1993, James Jordan, father and best friend of Michael Jordan, was murdered in his car on a country road in South Carolina.

The murder at first appeared to be a random slaying, but there were attempts by some media to tie James Jordan's murder to Michael's gambling debts. The combination of his father's death and constant media harping on his outside interests set Jordan on a surprise path.

According to reports that came out after the fact, Jordan had considered retirement prior to the events of the summer of '93. He had always had an interest in returning to his first athletic love, which was baseball, and he had accomplished a great deal already in basketball. Plus, he was receiving so much negative attention for his gambling that pressures seemed to be pushing him away from basketball. Then his father died.

The Bulls tried to talk him out of it. Bulls owner Jerry Reinsdorf had coach Phil Jackson talk to Jordan about a week before the announcement, but Jordan told Jackson he did not want to outstay his welcome, or be one of those players who played beyond his prime.

On October 5, late at night, news reports began to surface that Jordan was going to retire rather than return to the Bulls for the '93–94 season. Jordan had attended the White Sox game with Reinsdorf (who owned the White Sox as well) that night, and speculation was running rampant. Jordan made it official on October 6 at a media conference at the Berto Center, the Bulls' new practice facility in Deerfield.

The event was attended by hundreds of members of the Chicago and national media, as well as all of Jordan's teammates for the upcoming season. They included Toni Kukoc, the Croatian superstar who had been reluctant to come to America but finally agreed to do so for the chance to play with Jordan. Kukoc, who'd been abused by Jordan and Scottie Pippen during the '92 Olympic Games one year before he joined the Bulls, cried as Jordan made his announcement.

Jordan was only 30 years old at the time. While it was uncertain whether he would remain retired, the decision seemed to

Jordan Likes to Gamble

It was no secret Michael Jordan enjoyed gambling—cards mostly. He was a regular visitor to Las Vegas, and it was not an issue for anyone.

Until 1993, that is, when it was revealed that Jordan had been in Atlantic City into the early morning hours prior to a playoff game against the New York Knicks. Jordan had a poor game that night, going 12 for 32, and the Bulls lost their second straight in the series to go down 0–2. The Bulls eventually won the series, but the gambling story stuck with Jordan into the summer.

Other stories about Jordan's forays into gambling surfaced, including an entire book written by a man who allegedly gambled millions on the golf course with Jordan. The stories, plus the murder of Jordan's father in the summer of '93, prompted Jordan to retire from basketball in October '93.

One popular story about Jordan's fascination with gambling occurred in the '90 playoffs. The Bulls were playing Philadelphia in the second round, and the night after an off-day Jordan and a group of friends went to Atlantic City. They got back to the team hotel at about 7 AM, and Jordan ran into coach Phil Jackson, who was making his way to breakfast. Jackson asked Jordan why he was up so early and Jordan said "couldn't sleep." Then he went to his room, slept for a couple of hours before shoot-around practice, then slept again between the practice and the game. He scored 45 points that afternoon and led the Bulls to a 111–101 victory.

many an unfortunate turn of events for one of the great athletes of his time.

But Jordan did not stay away from professional sports for long. During the fall of '93, Jordan began working out in order to make an attempt to become a professional baseball player. Baseball was Jordan's first love as a child, and his father had played semi-pro ball growing up. Jordan was trying to achieve a childhood dream.

Jordan signed a contract to play for the Birmingham Barons, a AA affiliate of the Chicago White Sox. In '94, Jordan batted .202 with three home runs, 51 RBI, and 30 stolen bases for the Barons.

During the '94 season, the White Sox and Cubs played an exhibition game (this was prior to the introduction of interleague play, which allows the Cubs and Sox to play six games against each other each season). Jordan played for the White Sox, creating one of the greatest exhibition-game buzzes ever in Chicago. He got two hits in four at-bats.

During that summer, *Sports Illustrated* published one of its most famous covers. It was a picture of Jordan at the plate, along with the words "Bag It!" Jordan was extremely angered by the cover and the accompanying story and refused to speak with *Sports Illustrated* writers for years thereafter.

Jordan continued to play for the Scottsdale Scorpions of the Arizona Fall League in '94, but by that time he was plotting his return to basketball. His retirement from basketball ended in March '95, when he rejoined the Bulls at the end of the '94–95 season.

Bill Cartwright

Life works in mysterious ways.

Bill Cartwright, who played his college ball at the University of San Francisco in the long shadow of former Don (the team's nickname) Bill Russell, was almost selected by the Chicago Bulls in the 1979 draft. But the team already had a significant center in Artis Gilmore, so they chose David Greenwood instead.

Cartwright went to the New York Knicks as the No. 3 player in the draft and averaged more than 20 points per game his first two seasons with the team. But when popular center Patrick Ewing joined the team as the No. 1 pick in the 1985 NBA draft,

Cartwright's star began to shine less brightly. He also suffered numerous foot injuries that gave him a bad reputation in the highly critical Big Apple.

Cartwright had a reputation as a clumsy giant. He had sharp elbows that got him in trouble on a regular basis when he would get the ball in the post and try to swing around to assume a shooting position.

In the summer of 1988, Bulls general manager Jerry Krause traded popular power forward Charles Oakley to the New York Knicks for Cartwright. In the process, he irritated the Chicago media, who didn't understand the trade, and really angered Michael Jordan because Oakley was his best friend on the team.

But Cartwright was the defensive presence that Krause felt the Bulls needed in the middle. Cartwright was long, and Krause really liked long players. He was serious and strong-willed, and just wanted to win.

Offensively, Cartwright had a jump shot that started down by his hips, swung on a pendulum of two long arms, and then ended up high above his head. It looked like a giraffe's jumper. As a defensive presence, he took up a lot of room, and had more length than most players, making it hard to get a decent shot off from the lane.

Cartwright averaged 12.4 points per game his first season with the Bulls, but by the time they were winning titles, his scoring was down to 9.6 in 1991, 8.0 in 1992, and 5.6 in 1993. He averaged 5.1 rebounds per game during the championship years, when he was sharing playing time with Will Perdue and Stacey King in the middle.

More so than any other player on the first three-peat teams, Cartwright never developed a relationship with Jordan. They existed together on the court and succeeded, but rarely spoke off the floor. Cartwright was a quiet, introspective man while Jordan was an out-front media darling.

Cartwright had a distinctive, low-grumbly voice, which was impersonated by almost every teammate and Bulls fan in Chicago. Stacey King, the backup center for the Bulls and about 10 years younger than Cartwright, used to do his Cartwright impersonation on the team bus to the enjoyment of everyone but Cartwright.

While with the Bulls, Cartwright took an elbow to the throat during a game and suffered a damaged larynx. His already distinctive voice became even more gravelly.

Cartwright stayed with the team through the 1993 season. He eventually became the interim head coach of the Bulls late in 2001, coached the team the entire '02–03 season, and was fired during the '03–04 season.

Cartwright served as an assistant coach for both the New Jersey Nets and the Phoenix Suns after his time with the Bulls.

36 Scottie Pippen's Bad Times

Eventually, Scottie Pippen became the superstar teammate Michael Jordan needed to overcome the difficulties of being a one-man show. Together they claimed six NBA championships in the 1990s.

But that's not where Pippen started. Not by a long shot.

Pippen came from a family of 12 children in a dirt-poor existence in Hamburg, Arkansas. He was nothing special athletically in high school, but in his senior year he was the starting point guard for the team. However, since he stood just 6'1" and was from such a small area, he attracted no major college interest. In fact, in his junior year of high school he became team manager for the football team in order to make some money.

Pippen was invited to attend Central Arkansas on a federal grant to serve as the basketball team's manager. But by the time the spring semester of his freshman year rolled around, Pippen had grown to 6'3" and the Central Arkansas coach threw him on the team.

Pippen kept growing, as did his basketball talent. He became a two-time NAIA All-American at Central Arkansas. In his senior year, playing all over the floor, he averaged 23.6 points, 10 rebounds, and 4.3 assists. He shot 59 percent from the floor. He also had three-point range, hitting 58 percent from downtown. He received invitations to attend many of the pre-draft camps the NBA has to identify talent for the summer selection process.

This was not good news for Bulls general manager Jerry Krause, who was famous for finding unidentified talent. Pippen was his secret, and he was not happy that the secret was getting out.

So Krause engineered a draft-day deal with the Seattle SuperSonics, effectively selecting Pippen with the fifth pick of the 1987 draft.

While Pippen was developing a reputation among NBA scouts, no basketball fans had heard of him, and Krause had to explain just who Pippen was and what he could do. Early on, the best information Krause could offer was that Pippen had a huge wingspan and could cover ground quickly.

It took Pippen most of two years to get into the starting lineup (far more famous, but far less talented, Brad Sellers out of Ohio State was the starting small forward) but once he did, Jordan recognized that he had a running mate, someone who could match him on the offensive end and help out, maybe even dominate, on the defensive end.

Pippen, however, suffered forever as Robin to Jordan's Batman. No one ever invited comparisons, but comparisons came, and the comparisons were harmful to a player like Pippen, who came out of nowhere and had few professional expectations for himself.

His first bad moment came in the 1990 Eastern Conference Finals against the Detroit Pistons, when a lifelong problem with migraines hit him hard before Game 7 in Detroit. Pippen was nearly blinded by the pain, but played. He did not do well (two points and four rebounds) and was marked in the loss as soft. Jordan, it was said, would never be stopped by a simple migraine.

But Pippen became a star in the NBA the next year in the NBA Finals against the Los Angeles Lakers. The decision by coach Phil Jackson to have Pippen guard 6'9" point guard Magic Johnson disrupted both Magic and his teammates, and the Bulls cruised to their first title, beating the Lakers 4–1 in the best-of-seven series.

Pippen's next moment was an ignoble one. After winning three NBA titles, Jordan retired, and Pippen was left to carry on. The Bulls had acquired Croatian talent Toni Kukoc, and some thought maybe the Pippen-led Bulls could accomplish something without Jordan.

In the 1994 playoffs, the Bulls met the New York Knicks in the Eastern Conference semifinals. With the Bulls down two games to none and the score of Game 3 tied at 102, the Bulls had the ball with 1.8 seconds remaining. Jackson called a timeout and set up a play for Kukoc, using Pippen to inbound the ball and work as a decoy, hoping the Knicks would expect the ball to go back to Pippen. Pippen was so upset that he was not expected to take the last shot that he refused to go back into the game.

Kukoc hit the shot from 23 feet and the Bulls won the game. But Pippen had tarnished his good name, having a far more devastating effect than the migraine game had.

"I felt I should have been on the floor rather than inbounding the ball," Pippen said. "Fortunately, Kukoc hit the game-winner."

The Bulls lost to the Knicks that year, and then Jordan returned to the Bulls in the spring of 1995. The Bulls could not organize another title run until the full 1995–96 season, when Jordan and Pippen were reunited.

In 1996, the NBA decided to name the top 50 players in NBA history. Perhaps assisted by the recent memory of his dominant defensive performances and remarkable offensive development, Pippen was named one of the top 50 players, which was his greatest honor at the time.

After Jordan retired again in 1998, Pippen moved on as well, playing one year with Houston and four with Portland. He then returned to the Bulls to serve as a sort of on-court elder statesman. The plan didn't work, and the Bulls stayed one of the league's worst teams through the decade following the departure of Pippen and Jordan.

In 2010, the Bulls named Pippen a team ambassador, and he was present at almost every home game. In 2011, years after a statue had been erected in appreciation of Jordan, a half-body bust of Pippen was installed inside the United Center in honor of him. His No. 33 was retired in 2005.

37 John Paxson

John Paxson was not from Chicago. He was born in Ohio, played high school ball in Kettering, then became a name in Chicago when he attended the University of Notre Dame, playing for the Irish from 1980–83. He was a two-time All-America, averaging 16.4 points in his junior year and 17.7 points in his senior season. In his years at Notre Dame, he shot 52.6 percent from the field, most from the outside.

Paxson's father, Jim Paxson, played two seasons in the NBA in the mid-1950s. Paxson's older brother, Jim Jr., had made his way to the NBA (he played with Portland and Boston) while John was at Notre Dame.

Paxson was drafted 19th overall by the San Antonio Spurs and played there for two years in a backup role before signing a free-agent contract with the Bulls in 1986. He became the backcourt mate of Michael Jordan for most of the next seven seasons, finally losing his starting role during the 1993 campaign.

Paxson was a perfect backcourt partner to Jordan, standing out at the three-point line waiting for Jordan to find him after Jordan found his way to the basket impeded. But it took Jordan a while to realize Paxson could help him win games.

In one of the most famous, and perhaps apocryphal, moments in Bulls history, the Bulls were playing in Game 5 of the 1991 NBA finals against the Lakers. With the game tied at 93, Bulls coach Phil Jackson called a timeout. He looked at Jordan and said "Michael, who's open?" Jordan did not respond. Jackson asked the question again, this time with his hands on Jordan's shoulders. Jordan said, "Paxson," and Jackson said, "Then get him the ball." Paxson scored 10 points down the stretch of that game and the Bulls won their first NBA championship.

But it was in the 1993 season that Paxson had his greatest moment as a pro. He hit the game-winning three-pointer in Game 6 of the NBA Finals in Phoenix, a shot that propelled him to national fame. Although still in the shadow of Michael Jordan and Scottie Pippen, Paxson made an appearance on the *Late Show with David Letterman*, where he was celebrated for his feat.

After retiring as a player, Paxson spent one year as an assistant coach with the Bulls and won another ring with the '95–96 team. He then joined the Bulls broadcast team for several years, doing television color commentary, before he was hired by Bulls owner Jerry Reinsdorf in 2003 to become the team's vice president of basketball operations, replacing Jerry Krause, who resigned amid much criticism for his moves following the breakup of the dynasty in 1998.

Paxson rebuilt the Bulls through the first decade of the new century, adding players like Luol Deng, Ben Gordon, Kirk

Hinrich, and Joakim Noah before lucking into the No. 1 draft slot in 2009 and getting point guard Derrick Rose, a Chicagoan who played one year of college ball at the University of Memphis. By 2011, it appeared the Bulls would be battling for the Eastern Conference title for years to come.

 **The First Team**

The 1966–67 Bulls, the first team in franchise history, were put together by an expansion draft, a collegiate draft, and numerous trades.

The opening-day lineup included forwards Bob Boozer and Don Kojis, center Len Chappell, and guards Guy Rodgers and Jerry Sloan. Rodgers had been picked up in a trade with San Francisco in which the Bulls gave up Jeff Mullins, Jim King, and cash, something owner Dick Klein was not often inclined to do.

Despite reports that the team would never last in Chicago, and at least one public prediction that the lineup would not win 10 games all season, the Bulls won their first three games, beating St. Louis, San Francisco, and the Los Angeles Lakers. Rodgers scored 37 points in the franchise's first game, a 104–97 win over the Hawks. Rodgers had 34 points and 18 assists in the win over the Lakers that gave the Bulls a surprising 3–0 record.

The Bulls stayed above or near the .500 mark through the first 14 games before suffering a nine-game losing streak that left them at 7–15.

After going 4–1 in their first five games, the Bulls hosted the New York Knicks on October 23, 1966. The Chicago basketball fan base had grown quickly, and the Bulls hosted a crowd estimated at 10,000 in the 7,000-seat capacity Chicago Amphitheatre. Owner Dick Klein was finally told by fire marshals that he had to close the doors, and there were thousands of fans wanting to get in who could not do so.

The Bulls lost that game 124–105 before an announced crowd of 10,188.

During the first season, the city of Chicago saw one of the worst snowfalls in the city's history, including a night in which 26 inches of snow fell on the city. Attendance dropped rapidly through much of the winter, and one game had an announced audience of 1,077 when less than 100 people were estimated to be in the building to watch.

The Bulls did enjoy a little more success on the floor late in the season in order to get into the playoffs. They won eight of their last 12 games, including a 129–122 win over eventual champion Philadelphia, to reach the postseason.

Ben Bentley

The Bulls' first public relations man was Ben Bentley, a former boxing promoter from Chicago who was known as Benny the Burglar. The cigar-smoking people person was with the team from 1966 until 1973.

Bentley knew everybody in the Chicago media and he used all of his contacts to get the Bulls in the eyes of the city. He did everything he could to get fans into the seats and worked tirelessly from the beginning.

Bentley also served as the team's public address announcer in the first few years. He was an easy man to deal with because he let everything slide off his back. He had a great sense of humor and could call on that when he needed it.

When the team needed a mascot, they came up with the bull identity, and when the mascot needed a name, general manager Pat Williams named him "Benny" after Bentley.

"Without Benny, the team never would have had a chance to succeed in the city of Chicago," former Bulls general manager Jerry Krause said.

Both Rodgers and Sloan made the Western Conference All-Star team that year. Sloan averaged 17.4 points while Rodgers set an NBA record with 908 assists, breaking the mark previously held by basketball legend Oscar Robertson.

The Bulls went 33–48, setting a record for most wins by an expansion team. They made the playoffs and lost three straight games to the St. Louis Hawks in the first round. Johnny Kerr was named NBA Coach of the Year, one of the few ever to receive the honor while coaching a losing team. Rodgers led the team in scoring with 18 points per game and assists with 11.2, while Sloan led the team in rebounding with 9.1 boards per game despite playing shooting guard. Erwin Mueller, selected by the Bulls in the collegiate draft out of the University of San Francisco, was named to the NBA All-Rookie team while averaging 12.7 points.

The Bulls played those games at the Chicago Amphitheatre, the only year they played in the building.

Courtside seats for the Bulls games cost $4. The team played five games in Evansville, Indiana, where Sloan had played his college ball.

Dick Motta

John Richard Motta was born in Utah and was the coach at Weber State in Idaho when he was discovered by Bulls scout Jerry Colangelo. When Johnny "Red" Kerr resigned to join Colangelo with the expansion Phoenix Suns, Colangelo suggested Motta. Klein hired Motta because he wanted someone who knew how to teach and figured a college coach would be the perfect choice.

Coach Bob Biel

Do you remember the scene in the movie *Hoosiers* when Gene Hackman got himself tossed out of the game, turning the Hickory team over to assistant coach Dennis Hopper, who was not ready to coach?

Something similar happened to the Bulls during the 1973–74 season, when firebrand Dick Motta was coaching the team. He was doing so without an assistant coach when his backup Phil Johnson was hired to coach the Kansas City-Omaha Kings.

Before he could get around to finding a new assistant coach, Motta shoved a referee after a game and received a one-week suspension. Without an assistant coach to turn to, the Bulls allowed team trainer Bob Biel, a podiatrist by trade, to coach the team until Motta hired junior college coach Ed Badger as his assistant.

Motta wanted to win, but the Bulls of 1968–69 were operating on a shoestring budget, and Motta clashed with team owner Dick Klein throughout the season. The Bulls were rumored to be headed to St. Louis or Toronto because they were failing financially in Chicago, and through all that Motta was trying to win games.

Motta's first NBA team ended up 33–49 and failed to make the playoffs, the first time that had happened for the Bulls. But by his third year as coach, he led the Bulls to a 51-win season, won Coach of the Year honors, and the Bulls had four straight seasons of at least 50 wins.

Motta's legacy as a coach was cemented when the Bulls picked up Jerry Sloan and Norm Van Lier to play shooting guard and point guard, respectively. There has never been a more hard-nosed backcourt combination in NBA history than Sloan and Van Lier, and Motta fed off their defensive efforts, demanding similar play from the rest of the team.

At a time when teams were scoring 110 points per game on a regular basis, Motta coached a more defensive style. His Bulls teams with Sloan and Van Lier regularly finished near the top of the league in defensive numbers.

Unlike Kerr, who was a good-natured fellow, Motta was a fighter from the jump ball. He reportedly led the league in technicals on an annual basis, and once got four technicals in a game, forcing the league to change the rule regarding technicals, limiting players and coaches to two Ts before getting thrown out.

Motta had many special moments that represented his fiery nature, but few topped the night in Detroit when he drop-kicked the basketball and sent it into the upper deck at the Pistons' home, Cobo Arena. The referees (there were only two refs per game at the time) were busy dealing with personal fouls and a player battle on the floor and did not see it. Detroit coach Norm Van Breda Kolff ran onto the floor to complain about what Motta did, and Van Breda Kolff was thrown out of the game.

Another night, Motta was tossed from a game for throwing his jacket (one of those awful plaid jackets that were so popular in the mid-'70s) at a referee.

Motta coached the Bulls from 1968 to 1976. After leaving the Bulls at the end of the '76 season, he went on to coach the Washington Bullets, winning the NBA title in '78. He also coached Dallas, Sacramento, and Denver up until his retirement in 1997.

Motta finished his career with 935 wins. When Jerry Sloan was inducted into the Basketball Hall of Fame in 2009, he made an impassioned plea to get Motta inducted as well.

Motta's son, Kip, was an assistant coach in the NBA for four teams, twice working with his father in Dallas and Denver.

40 Jerry Sloan, the Player

Jerry Sloan was a farm boy from southern Illinois, and farm life in the mid-20th century was a place to learn how to work hard for what you wanted. That work ethic served Sloan well once he moved beyond the farm into the world of professional basketball.

After short stints at the University of Illinois and Southern Illinois, Sloan found a home at the more laid-back University of Evansville, which was an NCAA Division II school when Sloan arrived at the southern Indiana campus. While there, he led the Aces to two NCAA Division II championships, and his success as a player has never been matched. He averaged 15.5 points per game during his three years on the varsity, and the Aces were unbeaten in 1965.

Sloan could have been in the NBA that season. He was drafted as an eligible junior (because of his time at Illinois and SIU) in 1964 by the Baltimore Bullets, but Sloan elected to stay in school for his senior season with Evansville. That made him available again in the '65 draft and he was again drafted by the Bullets.

In '66, Sloan was selected by the Bulls in the expansion draft, but in the second week of the first season the Bullets contacted the Bulls to see if they could get Sloan back by way of trade. The Bulls said no, and the rest was NBA history in Chicago.

Sloan played 10 years for the Bulls and averaged 14.7 points over those seasons, but he was known more for his hard-working offensive style and his nearly invincible defensive presence. When the Bulls acquired Norm Van Lier in 1971 in a trade with Cincinnati, he and Sloan combined to be one of the most tenacious defensive guard duos in NBA history.

Sloan was named to the NBA All-Star team twice and was on the league's All-Defensive team four times.

Shortly after retiring due to a knee injury at the end of the 1975–76 season, Sloan became the first Bull to have his number retired. The No. 4 jersey still hangs in the United Center alongside those of Michael Jordan, Scottie Pippen, and Bob Love.

It was an indication of the type of player Sloan was that he led the team in rebounding his first season, with nine per game, while playing from the shooting guard position. He was named to the West All-Star team that first season, his second in the league.

In the Bulls' third season, 1968–69, Johnny "Red" Kerr was replaced as coach by Dick Motta, a hard-nosed man from Utah who had coached at Weber State in Idaho before becoming a pro coach. He loved defense, and when he saw Sloan play, he knew he had his shooting guard for a very long time.

In the '69–70 season, Sloan broke two ribs in a collision with Lew Alcindor of Milwaukee in the game's final minute. The Bulls had a game in Cincinnati the next night, and they were trying to reach the playoffs. Against the advice of team doctors, Sloan played against the Royals, even though he had to have help getting his jersey on. The Bulls won the game in overtime, advanced to the playoffs, and Sloan's legacy of toughness was well on its way.

41 Jerry Sloan, the Coach

Sloan retired as a player in 1976 after 11 years in the NBA. He was quickly recruited to be the head coach at the University of Evansville, but after five days on the job he withdrew from the position. Later that year, the entire Evansville team was killed in a plane crash.

Two years later, Sloan became a scout for the Bulls, then was quickly elevated to assistant coach, serving under Ed Badger, who had replaced Dick Motta after a disastrous '75–76 season. The Bulls went 31–51 in the '78–79 season under Larry Costello and Scotty Robertson, and local hero Sloan became the team's sixth head coach.

That year, the Bulls had the opportunity to get the No. 1 pick, dependent upon a coin flip with the Lakers. The Lakers won the coin toss and selected Magic Johnson, a 6'9" point guard out of Michigan State who had just won the NCAA Championship in a title game against Larry Bird's Indiana State. Johnson stated publicly numerous times that he would have much rather played for the Bulls, who were closer to home for him. The Bulls instead drafted David Greenwood out of UCLA, choosing him over center Bill Cartwright out of the University of San Francisco, who years later would end up a Bull.

Sloan's first Bulls team, which had a starting lineup of Greenwood, Scott May, Ricky Sobers, Reggie Theus, and Artis Gilmore, went 30–52. He coached the team in 1980–81, when they finished 45–37 and advanced to the playoffs for the first time in four seasons. They swept the Knicks in two games in the first round (which was best of three at the time) then were swept by the eventual champion Boston Celtics in the second round.

The '81–82 Bulls team added forward Orlando Woolridge to the squad and stayed close to the .500 mark through Christmas. By February, the team was 13 games under .500 when Sloan was fired and replaced by general manager Rod Thorn. Sloan finished his Bulls coaching career with a record of 94–121.

Sloan coached the way he played, in a straightforward manner. In '81, he decided free agent Larry Kenon wasn't playing with the effort he wanted, so he benched him and eventually stopped playing him, even though the Bulls had paid big money to have him join the club.

After leaving the Bulls following the '82 season, Sloan worked as a minor league coach (working for the Evansville Thunder of the Continental Basketball Association in '84) and an assistant coach with the Utah Jazz until '88 when he was named head coach, replacing longtime Jazz coach Frank Layden. Sloan remained coach of the Jazz until midway through the 2010–11 season, but never won an NBA title. His teams were beaten by the Bulls in the 1997 and '98 NBA Finals.

The Jazz made the playoffs in the first 15 seasons Sloan coached them, missing out in the 2004 season to end his streak. He ended his coaching career with the Jazz with a record of 1,127 wins and 682 losses, and was the only coach to win 1,000 games with the same franchise.

His last game as coach was against the Bulls on February 9, 2011.

He was inducted into the Basketball Hall of Fame in 2009, while still an active coach.

42 The Rodman Trade

During the late 1980s and early '90s, the Bulls had only one real rival, and that was the Detroit Pistons. The Pistons knocked the Bulls out of the playoffs in both 1989 and 1990, and knocked them out figuratively with their brutish style of play.

The Bad Boys were well-known and well-hated in Chicago. There was Bill Laimbeer, the brutish thug center; Rick Mahorn, the huge forward representing the immovable object; and Isiah Thomas, the former Chicago favorite turned traitor and Pistons' emotional leader.

Then there was Dennis Rodman, also known as "the Worm." He was a circus act, a sideshow, with his constant attempts to get into the head of his opponents, his wild leg kicks and insidious manner of getting rebounds, his hard-nosed, give-no-quarter defense. His multi-tattooed body and his occasionally bizarre behaviors fed into the dislike.

When Rodman pushed Bulls forward Scottie Pippen into the basketball stanchion in a 1991 playoff game, his status as Public Enemy No. 1 in Chicago was confirmed. He was the player Bulls fans most loved to hate. He was the antithesis of the Michael Jordan–led Bulls championship teams, which played with style and grace and comported themselves like classy competitors.

So it came as a complete shock when the Bulls announced the very secret deal that had been made with the San Antonio Spurs in the early fall of '95, just before the start of training camp. The deal sent backup center Will Perdue—a key member of the first three NBA titles—to the Spurs for Rodman, who had spent two seasons with David Robinson on the Texas team.

Rodman joined the Bulls having won four consecutive league rebounding titles, although he only played just over half of the games in the '94–95 season due to a suspension for refusing to play during a contract dispute he eventually lost. In his final season with the Spurs, Rodman was suspended for a playoff game in the Western Conference Finals for his behavior. That sealed the end of his tenure in San Antonio, one of the smaller markets in the NBA.

Bulls general manager Jerry Krause knew what he was doing when he made the deal. He was bringing the Bulls a rebounding marvel and a player of questionable character, or rather, unbelievably weird character. Because of the character concerns, Krause talked to head coach Phil Jackson and Rodman's potential future teammates Michael Jordan and Scottie Pippen before making the deal.

Jack Haley

Jack Haley? Who was Jack Haley?

Haley was a longtime bench-riding professional basketball player out of UCLA. How he got into the NBA is a good question (actually, he was drafted by the Bulls in 1988 and played 51 games for them that year). But how he stayed is a better question. He played very little throughout his career.

But he made friends with controversial forward Dennis Rodman when the two were together in San Antonio, and when the Bulls acquired Rodman from the Spurs in '95, they also signed Haley as a backup power forward. He also was assigned to be a watchdog for Rodman, whose behavior had gotten him into trouble on numerous occasions.

Haley was immediately placed on injured reserve, so he was with the team but not playing an active role. He played only in the 82nd game of the '95–96 season, when the Bulls set an NBA record with 72 wins.

Haley stayed with the Bulls for just the one season. By the time the '96 season ended, the Bulls appeared to have a handle on how to handle Rodman, and Haley's services were no longer needed.

Pippen initially said he did not think he would ever even speak to Rodman, a person he thought of every time he looked at his own face in the mirror and saw the scar from Rodman's infamous push years before.

"I don't think I will ever forget it," Pippen said following Rodman's introductory news conference.

When Rodman made his debut in Chicago in the fall of '95 as a member of the Bulls, he showed up for his introductory news conference with his short-cropped hair dyed red with the Bulls' logo dyed black on the back of his head.

No one knew at the time that Rodman would help the Bulls win three more titles. All they knew was that there was a new adventure in store for the future of the Bulls, and a new star had joined the team for the foreseeable future.

"If he's ready and willing to play, it will be great for our team," Pippen said. "But if he's going to be a negative to us, I don't think we need that. We could really be taking a huge step backward."

43 Three-Point Shootout

The NBA started jazzing up its All-Star Games in 1984 with the Slam Dunk contest, which was actually initiated in the American Basketball Association a few years earlier.

In 1986, the NBA added the three-point shooting contest to the All-Star Weekend list of events.

The Bulls have had three notable entries into the Three-Point Shootout over the years, including Michael Jordan.

The event calls for shooters to attempt five shots from each of five locations around the basket over a specific time period. In each round, they get a single point for each made shot and two points for each shot made with the last ball from each position. Those balls (called the money ball) are the red, white, and blue kind first used by the ABA.

Larry Bird of the Boston Celtics made the contest an instant hit. He won the contest each of the first three years of its existence, and added to his Larry Legend status one year when he entered the pre-event locker room and told everybody they would be shooting for second place.

Craig Hodges grew up in Park Forest, a Chicago suburb, and joined the Bulls in 1988, playing on the first two championship teams. He was a member of the Milwaukee Bucks for five seasons prior to joining the Bulls. He competed against Bird in those first three competitions.

Bird stopped competing after the 1988 contest, and Hodges, representing the Bulls in 1989, finished second to Dale Ellis of the Seattle SuperSonics. But over the next three years, Hodges dominated the event similar to the way Larry Bird dominated it in the early years.

Hodges won the competition in 1990 in Miami, 1991 in Charlotte, and 1992 in Orlando. In 1991, Hodges had the most amazing performance ever in the three-point shootout when he made 19 consecutive threes in one of the early rounds. The most any other player had previously managed in a row was 11 by Bird and Hubert Davis of the New York Knicks.

The consecutive shots record was one of the most dramatic moments in NBA All-Star Saturday history. With every shot Hodges made during the streak, the crowd got more and more excited, and Hodges clearly enjoyed the moment. (The streak is one of the more popular basketball clips watched on YouTube.)

In 1986, while playing with the Milwaukee Bucks, Hodges set a single-round high score of 25 points (points do not accumulate through rounds).

In 1994 in Minneapolis, both B.J. Armstrong and Steve Kerr of the Bulls participated. Kerr was a regular participant and won the event in 1997 in Cleveland.

In 1990, the All-Star Game was held in Miami. Michael Jordan, who had won the Slam Dunk contest two times in the early part of his career, begged out of the Slam Dunk that year. But to maintain his much-desired presence in All-Star Weekend festivities, he agreed to participate in the Three-Point Shootout.

He only made that mistake once, however, because he scored just five points in the first round that year, the lowest score ever achieved in the history of the Three-Point Shootout. The "achievement" was overshadowed because no-name boxer Buster Douglas upset Mike Tyson in a title bout that same night.

Toni Kukoc

In the late '80s and early '90s, the best international basketball team in the world was the Yugoslavian national team. While it was true the United States was able to pull together a team to win the Olympic gold medal in 1984, there was no question the best gathering of long-term talent was in Yugoslavia.

Yugoslavians Vlade Divac and Drazen Petrovic had come to the United States to play in the NBA before the Bulls selected Toni Kukoc in the 1990 NBA draft. They were both starters with their respective teams, and Petrovic in particular was turning into a star shooting guard in New Jersey.

Kukoc was a wunderkind, a 6'11" point forward with amazing abilities to score inside, shoot from outside, and pass the ball like "Pistol" Pete Maravich had done decades earlier. While Kukoc had many nicknames in Europe, Bulls general manager Jerry Krause liked to call him "The Waiter" because of his ability to deliver the ball to teammates where they could do the most damage.

When Krause made the selection of Kukoc, it was met with a dead silence among Bulls fans who knew little of his abilities and found out quickly he was not going to come to the United States right away. Krause was known for taking leaps of faith with his draft picks and going out of his way to find basketball talent, and the Kukoc signing was seen as just another day at the Bulls draft office.

Kukoc was reluctant to come to the United States. He was under contract with an Italian club team and was winning Italian championships on a regular basis. He was the biggest of the big, the most famous basketball player on the continent.

The Croatian Sensation,
Toni Kukoc (Triumph Books
collection)

Coming to the Bulls meant playing with Michael Jordan and Scottie Pippen, but it also meant taking a back seat to Jordan and Pippen. He was struggling with the idea even before Jordan and Pippen went out of their way to embarrass Kukoc during the 1992 Olympics, when the U.S. defeated Kukoc's Croatian team.

In between the 1988 and 1992 Olympic Games, Yugoslavia divided along historic cultural lines into Serbia and Bosnia. The Yugoslavian team broke up, and bad blood existed among lifelong friends. The war raging between the two new countries made life difficult even for those native Yugoslavians like Kukoc who spent little time at home.

Amid all that turmoil, Krause finally convinced Kukoc to come to the Bulls in the summer of '93, negotiating Kukoc free of his Italian contract. Months after arriving in the United States, as a stranger in a strange land, his dream of playing alongside Jordan died when Jordan announced his first retirement from basketball just before the start of the 1993 training camp. At the press conference announcing Jordan's decision, with all of Jordan's team-mates behind him, it was Kukoc who visibly cried.

Without Jordan to worry about, Kukoc had to find a way to curry favor with Pippen, who basically played the same position Kukoc did. The two had difficulty getting along, and matters only got worse when Bulls coach Phil Jackson called a game-winning play for Kukoc in a playoff game against New York in the 1994 Eastern Conference semifinal series. Pippen responded by refusing to re-enter the game, but Kukoc gained accolades from Chicago fans by hitting the game-winner anyway.

In his first NBA season, Kukoc averaged 10.9 points per game. His average grew to 15.7 points in his second season, when he ranked second to Pippen in scoring, rebounding, and assists. In the 1995–96 season, Kukoc realized his dream of playing with Jordan when His Airness returned to basketball. The Bulls then won three championships with Kukoc playing alongside his two former adversaries.

Kukoc averaged 13 points in all three of his title seasons and became a crowd favorite in Chicago. He stayed with the team for two more years following the breakup of the dynasty in 1998 before being traded to the 76ers. He played seven more years before retiring after the 2005–06 season, but remained in Chicago, where he raised his family.

The First Three-Headed Monster

With Jordan slashing into the lane and Scottie Pippen playing an inside-outside game, the Bulls did not need a dominant center to win. What they needed was someone to guard the other team's dominant center while providing some inside scoring and assistance running the vaunted Triangle Offense.

In the summer of 1988, when it appeared the Bulls were beginning a march toward title contention, Bulls general manager Jerry Krause angered Jordan by trading his best friend and teammate, Charles Oakley, to New York for Bill Cartwright, the gangly, sharp-elbowed center who had been bitten by the New York media. While Cartwright was ready to leave New York (the addition of Patrick Ewing had made his life difficult in the Big Apple), he entered another difficult position in Chicago: trying to find a way to appease and please Jordan.

Krause gave Cartwright backup in younger centers Will Perdue (a draft pick out of Vanderbilt) and Stacey King (a draft pick out of Oklahoma). Between the three of them, they offered 18 fouls to use against the likes of Akeem Olajuwon and Patrick Ewing. They were known as the three-headed monster.

Cartwright was a quiet, introspective man who at one time was considered a giant in the NBA in terms of his scoring ability. With the Bulls, his scoring was secondary. During the championship seasons, he averaged no more than 9.6 points per game, and that total dropped to 5.6 points during the 1992–93 season. His job was defense and distributing the ball from the post position in the Triangle Offense.

Perdue was a good-hearted guy with a strong work ethic but little to offer offensively. He, too, was in the game to play defense and pass the ball. He was the starting center for most of the games Cartwright missed due to his bad knees. Perdue ended up playing seven consecutive seasons for the Bulls. During the championship seasons he started 26 games and averaged between four and five points a game.

King was the anti-Cartwright. He was outgoing (he eventually became a broadcaster for the Bulls in the 2000s) and loved doing an impersonation of Cartwright's unique deep-gravelly voice. King was limited offensively because he could not use his right hand. The lefty averaged 8.9 points in the 1989–90 season, but that total dropped to five and six points during the championship seasons. He started 21 games during the championship seasons.

King's claim to fame came in Game 6 of the 1992 NBA Finals against the Portland Trail Blazers. He was part of a group of backups that entered the game with the Bulls down 17 points in the third quarter and Pippen the only starter remaining in. Joined by Bobby Hansen, B.J. Armstrong, and Scott Williams, King and Pippen pulled the Bulls back into the game, and in the fourth quarter the starters re-entered to win the game and the title.

During those first three titles, the Bulls had to deal with interior scoring threats such as Karl Malone, Ewing, David Robinson, and Brad Daugherty. The three-headed monster did the job on those guys well enough to allow Jordan and Pippen to pull the team to victory.

46 The Second Three-Headed Monster

When Michael Jordan made his return to basketball in spring 1995, Bulls general manager Jerry Krause was ready for him with a team that could vie for more NBA titles. Besides adding Toni Kukoc and other sundry pieces to the backcourt, he had the three centers he wanted to serve as the second three-headed monster.

In the summer of '93, after Jordan retired, Krause traded Stacey King to Minnesota for Luc Longley, a 7'2" Australian center out of the University of New Mexico. Will Perdue remained on the team, and Krause also acquired center Bill Wennington, a native

Canadian who played college ball at St. John's and was with the Sacramento Kings before joining the Bulls.

Longley is one of the great basketball heroes in University of New Mexico history. But his Australian roots came out in everything he did. He was relatively passive for a professional athlete (he was known as "the Affable Aussie") and very calm, although he could get his back up when provoked. He introduced the entire Bulls organization to Aussie speak, and soon everyone responded to questions with the reply "No worries, mate."

"He's not mean," Bulls coach Phil Jackson once said about Longley. "He's a solid worker, and he's very intelligent. But he's not mean. Some people think you have to have a center that's ferocious, that threatening type of defender."

Longley was a bit more dangerous offensively than some of his predecessors in the middle. During the championship years he averaged 9.1, 9.1, and 11.4 points, and his bulk created problems for opponents inside.

But like other centers before him, Longley could never fully curry favor with Jordan. To Jordan, centers in general were guys who stood in the way of the basket. He needed them to play defense on one end and get out of the way on the other.

During the 1996–97 season, Longley suffered an injury that could have only happened to him. On an off-day in Los Angeles before a game against the Clippers, Longley and teammate Jud Buechler, who had grown up in California, went bodysurfing. On what became his final trip in off the surf, Longley hit a sandbar hard with his shoulder and had to miss 20 games. He admitted he was afraid to tell coach Phil Jackson of the injury, although Jackson had always believed in allowing players to live lives outside of basketball on their days off.

Although Canadian at birth, Wennington was more Americanized than Longley, having attended St. John's University in New York. At seven feet tall, he was actually shorter than

Longley. As a player, Wennington was best known for his outside shot rather than his inside play. He was rarely a starter and rarely got a chance to show his abilities, but he had a big game in a contest against Houston one year and was nicknamed "Air Wennington" for his outside scoring threat.

Wennington stayed with the Bulls for six seasons. He averaged 7.1 points during the 1993–94 season when Jordan was in retirement. He started 47 games during the second three-peat years. He eventually wrote a book about his years with the Bulls titled *Tales from the Hardwood*.

During the second three-peat, the third member of the three-headed monster changed each year. It was veteran center James Edwards (known as "Buddha") in the 1995–96 season. For the 1996–97 season, Krause finally got to add longtime favorite Robert Parish (known as "The Chief") to the team. For the 1997–98 season, the third head belonged to veteran Joe Kleine, who provided muscle when needed.

By the time the second three-peat was having its run, the centers were dealing with Shaquille O'Neal, Tim Duncan, and Dikembe Mutombo, along with mainstays Patrick Ewing, David Robinson, and Alonzo Mourning. Again, they were best known for their use of the 18 fouls they had to offer each game.

47 It's Over

In the summer of 1998, the NBA and the players union were prepared to fight bitterly over a new collective bargaining agreement. The general consensus was that the entire 1998–99 season could be lost to the in-fighting.

Bulls GM Jerry Krause (left) and coach Tim Floyd (far right) watch Michael Jordan's retirement press conference on January 13, 1999. (Getty Images)

Bulls general manager Jerry Krause was ready to rebuild, although his intent was always to do it with Phil Jackson as coach and Michael Jordan as the star player. He was not going to be the man who chased Jordan away from Chicago, even though he believed he could build another championship roster when the time came to do so.

The relationship between Krause and Jackson had frosted over completely during the summer of '97, when Krause re-signed Jackson for one year and made it clear that it was only for the one season.

The contentious nature of the relationship was based in part on the fact that Jackson was getting so much acclaim for the team's success and Krause's opinion that Jackson was not grateful enough for Krause giving him the job in the first place back in 1990.

The relationship went dead cold in the summer of '97 when Krause's stepdaughter was married. Many of the Bulls' assistant coaches were invited to the wedding, as was Tim Floyd, a coach at Iowa State whom Krause had built a relationship with, but Jackson was not invited.

During the summer of '98, before it was announced Jackson would not return as coach, the Bulls hired Floyd to serve as director of basketball operations, moving him into a position on the team and serving notice that the team was ready to move on to the next phase.

As the Jackson situation played out, Michael Jordan reiterated his stance that he would retire himself rather than play for any coach other than Jackson. Meanwhile, the NBA Players Association wanted Jordan to take a leadership role in the fight against the league for the new collective bargaining agreement. Jordan, never much of a union guy, tried to remove himself.

Scottie Pippen was demanding a trade, believing the Bulls were never going to give him a contract similar to what Jordan had received over the years. Krause wanted to trade Pippen because of Pippen's complaints and to begin the process of building a new team.

In January 1999, the NBA and players union came to an agreement. Immediately, Jordan announced his retirement, and Krause signed Floyd to coach the Bulls. On January 21, it all became official. Dennis Rodman, Jud Buechler, and Steve Kerr were all released or traded. A day later Pippen was traded to Houston. One day after that, Luc Longley was traded to Phoenix. The Bulls got

Players Don't Win Championships

While the Bulls were winning championships, Bulls general manager Jerry Krause made a significant mistake. The details of the mistake are unclear, but the effect of the mistake was undeniable.

While the Bulls were winning the first three championships, Krause began to bristle because the players and coaching staff were getting all the praise. Krause had been lauded for selecting Scottie Pippen and Horace Grant in the same draft, and eventually fans came to realize getting Bill Cartwright for Charles Oakley was a good idea, but still, Krause felt some of the praise toward the championship team was missing the mark.

So Krause told somebody in the media, "Players don't win championships, organizations win championships." Bulls fans and players went berserk, thinking Krause was dissing the talented likes of Michael Jordan and Scottie Pippen, as if to say with the right organization, any players could win titles.

Unfortunately, Krause claims he was misquoted by one word. He says his statement was, "Players don't win championships alone; organizations win championships," and that word might have kept Krause out of trouble.

But the quote made the rounds without that extra word, and Krause was regarded as a man trying to claim personal triumph for the six NBA titles and disregarding the work of the players involved.

The stain from that quote colored the public perception of Krause until he retired in 2003.

nothing but tired veterans for any of those players, and the next era for the Bulls was underway.

With the season cut to 50 games, and the entire roster decimated, the Bulls went 13–37 in 1998–99 under Floyd. The players who remained from the second three-peat were Bill Wennington, Toni Kukoc, Ron Harper, Randy Brown, and Dickey Simpkins.

The Bulls did not again have a winning season until the 2004–05 campaign, long after Krause and Floyd had gone away.

48 Bob Love

Sometimes things just work out.

In November 1968, the Bulls traded Flynn Robinson, a point guard who had averaged 16 points for the team the previous year, to the Milwaukee Bucks for small forward Bob Love and guard Bob Weiss. The trade was necessary because Robinson could not get along with feisty Bulls head coach Dick Motta, who had threatened to quit if the team did not get rid of Robinson.

Bulls owner Dick Klein said he had already arranged the deal before Motta's demand, although he was not happy about giving up Robinson for two unknowns.

Love, a 6'8" forward who could shoot with either hand, was a quiet Louisianan from a large, financially strapped family. He played basketball at Southern University, and after earning All-America honors twice, he was drafted by the Cincinnati Royals in the fourth round of the 1965 NBA draft.

He did not make the team that year, but after being named Player of the Year in the minor league Eastern Basketball League, the Royals gave him a roster spot for two years as a backup. He was selected by Milwaukee in the '68 expansion draft that year, but was almost immediately traded to the Bulls.

The Bulls actually tried to trade Love twice before he worked his way into the starting lineup for Motta, who appreciated the quiet efficiency with which Love played the game.

In the '69–70 season, Love became a starter for Motta's Bulls and averaged 21 points and almost nine rebounds per game. Teammate Chet Walker, with whom Love formed one of the great forward tandems of the decade in the NBA, averaged 21.5 points per game for that team.

Bob Love is given the game ball after scoring his 10,000th-career point during a 1974 game against the SuperSonics.

In '70–71, Love surpassed Walker, averaging over 25 points per game (he ranked sixth overall in the league), leading the team to its first 50-plus-win season, and the next season he averaged almost 26 points, when the Bulls went an amazing 57–25. He made the NBA All-Star team three years in a row.

Love played four more full seasons for the Bulls, never averaging less than 19 points per game. Not until the '76 season did he suffer through a losing season with the team.

Amazingly, Love's entire career, his entire life, was hampered by a severe stutter. The Milwaukee Bucks traded him initially because he could not talk and therefore could not help promote the team. When his Chicago playing days ended and he tried to get basketball work, he was shunned because of his speech impediment.

Because he did not make a great deal of money in his playing days, and because his stutter affected his ability to get work, he ended up working very low-paying jobs. He eventually got a job at Nordstrom in Seattle (where he had spent his last days as a player), working on the lowest level of the company ladder as a busboy and dishwasher in the company lunchroom.

An executive at Nordstrom decided to pay for Love's speech therapy, and Love eventually was able to speak properly. Later on, the Chicago Bulls hired him as director of community services, which required him to make hundreds of speeches a year to youth and community groups in the Chicago area.

Love's No. 10 jersey was retired by the Bulls in 1994.

49 Bulls In the Olympics

Throughout the 20th century, the International Olympic Committee seemed to have consistent trouble distinguishing professional athletes from amateurs. Basketball, gymnastics, hockey, and swimming were among the sports most affected by the constant conversation as to whether Olympic athletes were amateur (as they were supposed to be) or professional (which many were).

Eventually, the IOC sort of gave up fighting that fight.

Through the 1988 Summer Olympics in Seoul, South Korea, Olympic basketball players were supposed to be amateur. The United States was sending its best collegiate players, and from 1936 to 1976, they won all but one gold medal (and were cheated out of the one they lost in 1972).

The U.S. boycotted the 1980 games in Moscow, won the gold in basketball in 1984, but in 1988 finished in third place with a team that included future NBA players such as David Robinson, Mitch Richmond, Danny Manning, and Dan Majerle. That year, the Soviet Union beat the Yugoslavian national team in the final, while the United States settled for the bronze by beating Australia.

Believing they were not competing on a level playing field with the Eastern European teams, whose players were, for all intents and purposes, professionals, the U.S. led a campaign to open the basketball competition to all players. Then, in 1989, the IOC finally agreed. Professional players would be allowed to play in the 1992 Olympic Games in Barcelona.

So for the 1992 Games, the U.S. put together a collection of talent that came to be known as "The Dream Team." Michael Jordan and Scottie Pippen were members of a team that included 11 eventual Hall of Fame players. Magic Johnson of the Los

Michael Jordan, Patrick Ewing, and Scottie Pippen cheer on fellow members of The Dream Team during the 1992 gold medal game against Croatia.

Angeles Lakers and Larry Bird of the Boston Celtics were the elder statesmen on the team, but the club also had Chares Barkley, Chris Mullin, Patrick Ewing, Karl Malone, John Stockton, David Robinson, Clyde Drexler, and one collegian, Christian Laettner. The team was coached by Chuck Daly, who had been the coach of the two-time NBA champion Bad Boy Detroit Pistons of the late '80s and early '90s.

The United States team was so dominant in all of its games that Daly never had to call a timeout during the tournament. The United States won the 1992 championship game 117–85 over Croatia. On the Croatian team was Toni Kukoc, who would become a member of the Bulls in the summer of '93, helping the team win three championships from 1996–98.

Jordan and Pippen were unhappy with the attention Kukoc garnered from Bulls general manager Jerry Krause, who drafted Kukoc in 1991 and praised his skills so much it sounded as if he was a combination of Jordan and Pippen. The Bulls/Olympians made it a mission to keep Kukoc from having a good game in the gold medal contest, and Kukoc ended up with seven turnovers and four points on 2-for-8 shooting.

Pippen was on the United States team again in 1996 in Atlanta, and it beat the Yugoslavian team 95–69 in the gold medal game. That team won all of its games by an average margin of 31 points.

Blossoming Bulls superstar Derrick Rose played for the FIBA World Championship team that went undefeated in Turkey in 2010, and was expected to be a starter for the 2012 Olympic team before he tore his ACL in the first round of the NBA playoffs. Luol Deng, despite a wrist injury, was scheduled to play for England during those same London Olympics.

Players who eventually became Bulls who played in the Olympics include Scott May, Joe Kleine, and Carlos Boozer. Doug Collins, who coached the Bulls from 1986–89, played for the ill-fated '72 team.

50 The Year Jordan Wasn't MVP

Michael Jordan won his first NBA MVP award for the 1987–88 season, when he averaged 35.0 points and shot 53.5 percent from the field. That year he led the Bulls to a 50–32 record, their best since the team won 45 games in 1981. The NBA MVP is for regular season excellence. The league awards an MVP for the NBA Finals as well.

It was Jordan's fourth year in the league. The previous three awards had gone to basketball legends Larry Bird ('85 and '86) and Magic Johnson ('87). Johnson won it again in both 1989 and 1990, but Jordan won his second MVP in 1991 and then won again in 1992.

Charles Barkley of Phoenix won in 1993 and deserved it as the Suns had the best record in the NBA that year thanks to him. Then Jordan retired for most of the next two seasons, and the MVP went to Hakeem Olajuwon of Houston in '94 and David Robinson of San Antonio in '95.

In 1995–96, the Bulls set an NBA record for victories with 72, and Jordan, who had made a successful comeback from retirement, baseball, and an embarrassing performance in the '95 playoffs, earned his fourth MVP award. That year he averaged 30.4 points, to lead the league. He was also named NBA All-Defensive First Team, as well as winning his fourth NBA Finals MVP Award.

In 1996–97, Jordan averaged 29.6 points and led the Bulls to 69 victories, tying the former record for wins in a season, which the Bulls had erased with their 72 wins the year before. But that year Karl Malone of Utah averaged 27.4 points, shot a career-best .550 percent from the field, and led the Jazz to a team-best 64 wins, the best in the Western Conference.

In an election-day upset of momentous importance, Malone outpolled Jordan for the MVP award.

The Deseret News, a newspaper in Salt Lake City, had taken a straw poll by phone of all the voters for the MVP, of which there were three in each NBA city. The newspaper was the first to reveal that all three voters in Chicago—Terry Armour of the *Chicago Tribune,* John Jackson of the *Chicago Sun-Times,* and I (*Daily Herald*)—had voted for Malone.

Jordan accepted the announcement with aplomb, saying that if he had had a vote that year, he would have voted for Malone as well. But the Chicago writers were vilified in letters to the editor and on sports radio for several weeks thereafter.

There was a belief that many people voted for Malone in 1997 because they were just tired of voting for Jordan. Jordan had won the award in 1988, 1991, and 1992, and came in second in 1993 to Charles Barkley of Phoenix, in another example of voting against the favorite. That year Jordan averaged 32.6 points but lost to Barkley, who averaged 25.6.

In 1997–98, Jordan was again named the league's MVP, his last such award. He retired again at the end of the 1998 season. He won the award five times over a stretch of 11 seasons and he essentially did not play in two of those seasons. The only player with more MVPs is Kareem Abdul-Jabbar with six, while Bill Russell earned five.

In 1994, when Jordan was retired, Bulls forward Scottie Pippen finished third in the MVP balloting behind Hakeem Olajuwon and David Robinson.

In 2011, Derrick Rose became only the second Bulls player to win the MVP award.

51 The Jordan Statue

On the east side of the United Center stands the most consistent reminder of the greatness of Michael Jordan.

A 12-foot-tall bronze statue, depicting Jordan leaping into the air toward a dunk over the outstretched hand of a defender and the head of another, stands outside the east entrance to the United Center's offices. It is the single most visited spot reminding fans of the greatness and significance of Michael Jordan.

The statue was designed by Omri and Julie Rotblatt-Amrany, a couple from Jordan's Chicago hometown of Highland Park, a northern suburb. The statue was unveiled on November 1, 1994, before a national television audience on a taping of the *Larry King Live* show, the same night Jordan's No. 23 was retired by the Bulls in a UC ceremony. The United Center had opened just three months prior to the statue's unveiling. The building itself is known as "The House That Jordan Built."

The 12-foot statue sits upon a five-foot black granite cube (making the entire structure 17 feet tall), which is inscribed with a list of many of Jordan's NBA statistical accomplishments. There is also the inscription: "The best there ever was. The best there every will be," which is not attributed to anyone.

The statue and base weigh approximately 2,000 pounds. The depiction of Jordan taking to the air is attached to one of the defenders only at Jordan's knee. The rest of Jordan's form is unattached, making the statue seem even more representative of Jordan's ability to fly above his competition.

The Jordan statue is a favorite stop for tourists visiting Chicago. Before Bulls games, the line for photos runs deep and often continues well past the start of the game.

During the Chicago Blackhawks' Stanley Cup run in 2010, the Jordan statue was adorned with a jersey of Blackhawks captain Jonathan Toews and a hockey helmet. There were also ice skates on Jordan's feet, which are far spread and hang out beyond the edges of the statue's base.

The perpetual leap, frozen on the east side of the House That Jordan Built.

Gate 3½

On the west side of Chicago Stadium, a single door went from the team parking lot into the first floor of the building. It was Gate 3½, and it was the player, coach, and media entrance to the stadium.

Guarded by security, it was still a very public and visible entrance. Fans could stand beyond the parking lot and call out to the players as they walked into the building.

When the United Center was built to replace the Stadium, Gate 3 ½ was moved to the northeast corner of the building. It was used for media and other ancillary gameday personnel. Players enter the United Center from the parking lot inside the outer shell of the stadium.

When Jordan's statue was unveiled in 1994, it sparked a massive development of Chicago sports history statues. Suddenly, all of the pro sports teams in Chicago started putting up statues of their best players or favorite people.

The Chicago Cubs now have statues of former players Ernie Banks and Billy Williams outside Wrigley Field, as well as statues of former broadcasters Harry Caray and Jack Brickhouse. The Chicago White Sox have sculptures of players Minnie Minoso, Carlton Fisk, Luis Aparicio, Nellie Fox, Billy Pierce, and Harold Baines, as well as former owner Charles Comiskey.

The Chicago Blackhawks, not to be outdone by the Jordan statue, erected statues to former star players Bobby Hull and Stan Mikita that stand on the west side of the United Center.

In 2011, the Chicago Bulls unveiled a half-body bust of Bulls forward Scottie Pippen and placed it inside the United Center on permanent display on the building's west side.

52 Norm Van Lier

Bring up Norm Van Lier's name to Bulls fans and see how agitated people get. No player stirred the spirits of Bulls fans early in the franchise's history more than Stormin' Norman.

Van Lier was an amazing all-around athlete. He played football, baseball, and basketball in high school. He also received offers to play baseball and was even recruited to play college football, but no one would offer him a chance to play quarterback.

Instead, he went to tiny St. Francis College in Pennsylvania to play point guard. His concentration in basketball was on defense, but he still received enough notice from NBA scouts that he was drafted by the Chicago Bulls in the third round of the 1970 draft. He was immediately traded to Cincinnati, where he played for coach Bob Cousy, the Hall of Fame point guard from the previous generation. Under Cousy's tutelage, Van Lier led the NBA in assists in 1970–71 for the Royals. The Bulls reacquired him 10 games into the '71–72 season, and he eventually earned three All-Star nods in his seven seasons with the team.

Van Lier and all-star (and future Hall of Fame coach) Jerry Sloan played together in the Bulls backcourt until Sloan retired following the '75–76 season. Together they formed one of the nastiest defensive duos in basketball history. But they also had a preseason fight against each other when Van Lier was with the Royals and Sloan was with the Bulls. When the opportunity came to reacquire Van Lier, the team asked Sloan if he could play with the guy, and Sloan said he appreciated Van Lier's willingness to scrap.

The 1971–72 team, with Sloan and Van Lier at the guard spots, was the No. 1 defense in the league, allowing just 102.9

Norm Van Lier drives past Philadelphia 76er (and future Bulls coach) Doug Collins on his way to the basket.

points per game at a time when teams were regularly scoring over 110 and 120 points a game.

Van Lier was more of an assist guard than a scoring guard. He averaged 11.8 points and 7.0 assists in his career. He was named to the NBA's All-Defensive First Team three times and the Second Team five times. He was named to the All-NBA Second Team once in 1974. In the 1974–75 season he had his highest scoring average as a Bull, 15.0 points per game.

After retiring in 1979, Van Lier tried his hand at coaching but never got a bite of the apple at the NBA level. He spent one year in Worchester, Massachusetts, coaching a minor-league team, as well as a high school team that reached the title game in its division.

From 1992, he rejoined the Bulls family (in a way), working as a pre- and postgame TV analyst for Bulls games. Van Lier was always a showman as well as an athlete, so it is no surprise that he appeared in two movies, *Barbershop* and *Barbershop II*.

Van Lier's love of the Bulls, and his adamant on-air demands that the team play hard-nosed defense the way he did decades earlier, made him popular with fans who never saw him play. There was a regular call for Van Lier's jersey No. 2 to get retired, but it never happened.

Van Lier was 61 years old when he was found dead in his Chicago apartment on February 26, 2009. On that same day, former Bulls coach and popular broadcaster Johnny "Red" Kerr died.

53 Derrick Rose, the Rookie

When he was general manager of the Chicago Bulls, Jerry Krause had a lot of rules regarding player selection. One of them was that the player could not be from the city of Chicago. Too much baggage, Krause would say, too many people wanting to pull the player away from the team, too many hangers-on, too many ticket requests, too much pressure to succeed.

He actually violated his own rule twice. The first time was when he picked up Randy Brown from Sacramento in 1995, and Brown became a key second-string component to the second three-peat teams from '96–98. But Krause explained Brown's addition by saying he had been in the league and out of Chicago for five years and had already sowed his wild oats, so to speak. Brown was grounded.

Krause violated the rule again in '01 when he selected center Eddy Curry from Thornwood High School. Curry, a giant of a man with absolutely no work ethic, never worked out, and that draft, in which he also acquired high-schooler Tyson Chandler, ended up being Krause's downfall in Chicago.

Seven years later, the Bulls had the No. 1 pick in the '08 NBA draft and used it to select Simeon High School star Derrick Rose, who had grown up in one of the toughest neighborhoods on Chicago's south side. He went to college for one year at the University of Memphis, but he was from Chicago, no question about it.

Whatever concern might have existed about bringing Rose to the team he had grown up watching and admiring was negated by his very strong family and upbringing. Rose's mother, Brenda, raised four sons by herself, and Rose was known for both his humble nature and strong work ethic.

Rose was joining a team with a strong backcourt already. Ben Gordon, a long-range shooter, was the team's leading scorer. Luol Deng was a talented small forward, and Kirk Hinrich was a Kansas product with ball-handling and shooting capabilities.

Rose was immediately placed in the starting lineup with Gordon, while Hinrich became a sixth man. In his first season,

Rose averaged 16.8 points per game, shot 47.5 percent from the field, averaged more than six assists a game, and showed glimpses of the player he was going to become.

Rose became the Bulls' first rookie since Michael Jordan to score in double figures in his first 10 games. There was a push to get him considered for an All-Star bid in his first season, but he did not get chosen. However, he did play in the All-Star Game Rookie Challenge and won the Skills Challenge, a competition between invited players of any experience level, not just rookies. The skills challenge required skill in passing, dribbling, and shooting.

A late push by Rose and the Bulls got the team into the play-offs. Rose won the Rookie of the Year award, beating out O.J. Mayo of Memphis. The only other Bulls to win the award were Michael Jordan in 1985 and Elton Brand in 2000.

With a record of 41–41 in '09, the Bulls ended up paired against the Boston Celtics in the first round of the playoffs. The Celtics were the second seed in the East, and the Bulls were the seventh. But the Bulls, led by Rose and second-year center Joakim Noah, gave the Celtics the best battle of the first round, extending the series to seven games. Four of the seven games went into overtime, the first time any playoff series in the NBA had required four extra-period games.

In the first game of the series, Rose scored 36 points. That tied the NBA record for points scored by a rookie in his first playoff game (Kareem Abdul-Jabbar, 1970). Rose also had 11 assists in that game, and the Bulls won 105–103 to upset the Celtics on their own floor.

Rose's performance in his rookie season prompted general manager John Paxson to let Gordon go to the Detroit Pistons as a free agent in the summer of 2009.

54 Rod Thorn

In 1978, the Bulls were in major rebuilding mode. Ed Badger left as coach, their talent from the Motta era was all but gone, and outside of Artis Gilmore, their roster was filled with a bunch of effort guys with little talent.

The Bulls hired Rod Thorn, an assistant coach with the New Jersey Nets, to serve as their new general manager. Thorn played at West Virginia University and had eight years in the NBA before going into coaching. Thorn would eventually be responsible for two significant draft picks in Bulls history.

Thorn was a highly rated college player, selected second overall by the Baltimore Bullets in the 1963 NBA draft. He ended up playing for four teams in his NBA career before getting into coaching. He was head coach of the Spirits of St. Louis of the American Basketball Association for the first half of the 1975–76 season, but was fired after a 20–27 start.

Thorn's first NBA draft pick as general manager of the Bulls was the 1978 selection, when the Bulls picked Reggie Theus out of the University of Nevada Las Vegas over future NBA stars Maurice Cheeks and Michael Cooper. For a coach, Thorn decided not to promote popular assistant coach and former Bull Jerry Sloan. Instead he hired Larry Costello, who had coached the Milwaukee Bucks to the NBA title in 1971, with Kareem Abdul-Jabbar in the middle.

Costello did not last the entire season. He was accustomed to a half-court set offense and Theus wanted to run the ball up the floor as he had done at UNLV. Thorn hired Scotty Robertson to be interim coach with the intention of giving the head job to former Bulls star Jerry Sloan at the start of the 1979–80 season.

Before there was a draft lottery, the two teams that were the worst in their conferences would flip a coin for the first pick, and in 1979 those teams were the Bulls and the New Orleans Jazz, who had already traded their first round pick to the Los Angeles Lakers. Thorn, representing the Bulls, made the call in the coin flip for the No. 1 draft pick, which was expected to be star point guard Magic Johnson from Michigan State. Thorn called "heads" (he chose heads because that was what fans voted for in a phone poll the team conducted), the coin came up tails, and the Lakers got to select Johnson, who went on to win five NBA championships and have a Hall of Fame career with that team. The Bulls selected David Greenwood out of UCLA, and Greenwood played six seasons with the Bulls before finishing his career with the Spurs.

Thorn finally hired Jerry Sloan to coach the Bulls, and then fired him during the 1981–82 season. Thorn then decided to coach the team himself before turning the reins over to run-and-gun coach Paul Westhead for one season. Thorn left the team when the ownership changed over to Jerry Reinsdorf's group in 1985.

Thorn immediately became the NBA executive VP of basketball operations from 1986 to 2000. He then became general manager of the New Jersey Nets in 2000, winning Executive of the Year in 2002 when the Nets made the NBA Finals. As of 2012 he is the acting president of the Philadelphia 76ers.

Reggie Theus

Selected out of UNLV in 1978, Reggie Theus hit Chicago running. A stylish, flashy player, Theus lived near Chicago's famed party district of Rush Street and became known for his lifestyle as well as his playing ability.

Theus was a star from his days with the Runnin' Rebels of UNLV. The team was one of the highest-scoring teams in collegiate history, setting records for points and field goals during the 1977 season. They reached the NCAA Final Four that year, losing to North Carolina in the semifinal game.

After feeding on a workmanlike team that included thrashers like Jerry Sloan and Norm Van Lier, Theus was a wakeup call to Chicago.

Theus had difficulty with his teammates throughout most of his tenure with the Bulls because he was the star and there was not much else to the team. But Theus did bring attention to the team, scoring 18.8 points in his five and a half years with the team, including the 1982–83 year when he averaged 23.8 points per game. He made the All-Star team twice.

In his rookie campaign, Theus averaged 16.3 points per game and finished second in the Rookie of the Year balloting behind Phil Ford out of North Carolina, whom Theus had competed against in college. Theus averaged 20.2 points in his second season, but continued to struggle under Coach Sloan, who wanted Theus to concentrate on defense. Theus had simply never needed to do that before.

For the 1983–84 season, the Bulls hired Kevin Loughery to coach. Loughery, who had won two titles in the ABA and was a winning coach with Atlanta in the NBA, did not appreciate the fact that Theus held out for a better contract at the start of the season. Theus played very little once he came back, and when fans would call out for Theus to play, he would wave a towel over his head from his bench seat to incite them further.

Midway through the 1983–84 season, Theus was traded to Kansas City, effectively making room for a high-flying shooting guard named Michael Jordan.

After ending his NBA career with stints with the Atlanta Hawks, Orlando Magic, and New Jersey Nets, Theus became a coach. He coached New Mexico State into the NCAA tournament and later coached the Sacramento Kings. He interviewed to become head coach of Chicago's DePaul Blue Demons as well.

By the time his playing career ended, he was one of only four players to have accumulated at least 19,000 points and 6,000 assists. The others were Hall of Famers Oscar Robertson, Jerry West, and John Havlicek.

Jerry Reinsdorf

In 1984, many of the Bulls ownership group had tired of the business and wanted to sell. They lost millions of dollars over the years and were no longer interested in losing more.

Jerry Reinsdorf, owner of the Chicago White Sox, found out from New York Yankees owner George Steinbrenner that some of the Bulls owners were ready to sell. Steinbrenner was a part owner of the Bulls. Reinsdorf, a Brooklyn native with a love of baseball and the New York Knicks, made his fortune in real estate investment. He was interested in adding the Bulls to his White Sox ownership.

Reinsdorf created an ownership group of 24 investors and purchased a majority share of the Bulls in winter 1985, during Jordan's first season with the team. At the press conference announcing the sale, Reinsdorf promised to be the ownership face of the franchise, which he was.

"If what I was thinking about was making a return on investment, there are a lot of other things smarter than this. But why does anyone own a sports club? They like the sport, they like to be involved in it, and it's a way of making a contribution to the community."

When he took over, Reinsdorf was appalled at the state of the team. Even though the previous ownership group was comprised of very wealthy men, they operated the Bulls on a shoestring budget. The Bulls were still practicing at Angel Guardian gym, their offices were small, and the team had no sales or marketing division.

So Reinsdorf started to rebuild the team. His first step was to relieve Rod Thorn of his duties, replacing him with Jerry Krause, who became vice president of basketball operations. They had an

Grant Park

Grant Park is a huge tract of land in Chicago, south of the famed Loop Business District. It is bordered by Michigan Avenue on the west and Lake Michigan on the east. It is one of the great American urban parks.

It was also home to the Bulls' six NBA championship celebrations. Every time the Bulls won a title, thousands of fans would gather in front of a specially constructed stage to hear speeches from all of the players and coaches, as well as owner Jerry Reinsdorf.

The Grant Park celebrations were often criticized, however, simply because they weren't parades. In most American cities, professional sports teams had parades. But Reinsdorf decided it would be prudent to have a single-spot celebration, and it became a tradition that was revisited year after year, championship after championship.

However, when the Chicago White Sox (also owned by Reinsdorf) won the World Series in 2005, the team had a parade through the downtown city streets rather than a Grant Park celebration.

For the first title, the crowd in Grant Park was estimated at between 500,000 and 1 million.

After the second title, Scottie Pippen made the comment that got everyone thinking about the future possibilities. "Let's go for a three-peat," Pippen said to cheers from the crowd.

incredibly strong relationship that served the Bulls well as they built a team around Michael Jordan.

Reinsdorf moved the team's practices from Angel Guardian gymnasium to a private health club in Deerfield called the Multiplex. The team used the general-purpose basketball floor and the strength and conditioning equipment until constructing their own building, the Berto Center, in 1992.

With the growing fame that came with Jordan's increased popularity, Reinsdorf started chartering flights for the club, which had been flying commercial like all other teams.

Reinsdorf was known for his loyalty to those who were loyal to him. He named the Bulls' practice facility after his longtime personal assistant, Sheri Berto, when she died unexpectedly in 1991.

When Jordan retired in 1993, he allowed the star basketball player to pursue his original dream of being a professional baseball player, setting him up with the Birmingham Barons in Double-A (a White Sox affiliate) for the summer of '94.

When Krause fired Doug Collins as coach of the Bulls in summer 1989, Reinsdorf announced that it was his decision, not Krause's. In his press briefings regarding the firing, Reinsdorf made the famous case that Collins had brought the team from Point A to Point B but was not the person to take the team to Point C, which was a championship.

When Jordan returned from his first retirement to play in the 1995–96 season—on his way to a second three-peat of championships for the Bulls—he was given a new contract for $30 million a year, making him the highest-paid basketball player ever. At the time of the signing, Reinsdorf remarked that he would regret giving Jordan such a lucrative contract, stating his belief that no basketball player was worth $30 million a year.

Reinsdorf and Blackhawks owner William Wirtz combined to throw $175 million at the project that became the United

Center, the new home for the Bulls and Blackhawks, directly across Madison Street from Chicago Stadium, which was torn down.

As owner of the Chicago White Sox, Reinsdorf had great influence over Major League Baseball. He reportedly had a role in deciding which ownership group would be allowed to purchase a number of teams, and he battled with former Major League Commissioner Fay Vincent until Vincent was removed from the position in 1992. He helped get former Milwaukee Brewers owner Bud Selig installed as commissioner after Vincent.

Reinsdorf negotiated the deal that allowed his White Sox to move from old Comiskey Park into a new, modern stadium that eventually became known as U.S. Cellular Field, even going so far as threatening to move the team to Florida in order to get the deal he wanted.

57 The Shot (Cleveland)

Before they hated the Detroit Pistons, before they hated the New York Knicks, the Chicago Bulls had a tumultuous relationship with the Cleveland Cavaliers.

The rivalry was borne out of the teams being so close in terms of talent. In 1988, the Bulls finished second in the Central Division with 50 wins and the Cavaliers were fourth with 42 wins, but the Central Division was probably the best division in basketball at the time.

The Bulls had home-court advantage in the first round of the playoffs against the Cavaliers in 1988 and won the series in the deciding Game 5 at home, 107–101. The home team had won every game in the series. It marked the first time the two teams had met in the postseason, but not the last.

In 1989, the Bulls and Cavaliers were again thrown together, but this time the Cavaliers had the home-court advantage and the confidence that it would be enough to get them into the second round. The Cavaliers had beaten the Bulls in all six regular-season meetings that season.

The Bulls stole home-court with a seven-point win in the opener, but with the series on the line in Game 4 at Chicago Stadium, the Cavaliers beat the Bulls in overtime 108–105. Jordan missed two key free throws in the final minute of that game that allowed the Cavaliers to steal the win.

That set up Game 5 at Richfield Coliseum, outside of Cleveland. The game was close, and the lead changed hands nine times in the final three minutes. With six seconds remaining in the game, Michael Jordan hit a 12-foot jumper to put the Bulls ahead 99–98, but Craig Ehlo of Cleveland, an outside scoring threat, made a surprise layup with three seconds remaining to put the Cavaliers back ahead, with only three seconds left on the clock.

The Bulls set up a play, with Brad Sellers throwing the ball in to Jordan, who caught the ball between Ehlo and Cleveland teammate Larry Nance. Ehlo made a swipe at the ball, allowing Jordan to dribble to his left, getting to the middle of the key, where he leapt, launching a high-arcing 16-foot shot over the outstretched hands of Ehlo. The shot went through the basket, the Bulls won, and then bedlam ensued.

Jordan hit the ground on his feet, triple-pumped his fists sideways, and then jumped into Sellers' arms. Collins ran past assistant coach Phil Jackson in a wild circle on the floor, celebrating as if the Bulls had won something significant.

It became known as "The Shot" and has been replayed millions of times whenever Jordan's performance at clutch time needs some demonstration.

Jordan finished the game with 44 points, but more than that, he had added a key component to his resume. His reputation as a last-second game-nailer was solidified.

"This is probably the biggest shot I have hit in the NBA," Jordan said. "When we lost after I missed that last free throw and last shot, it was the lowest I've ever felt in basketball."

Jordan said the shot was more significant than the basket he made to win the 1982 NCAA Championship for North Carolina.

The Cavaliers fell apart after that and did not see basketball success until the late 2000s, when they acquired LeBron James and made it to the NBA finals in 2007.

58 The Detroit Pistons

There were Eastern Conference teams Michael Jordan and the Bulls most enjoyed tormenting. Over the years, they had significant rivalries with the New York Knicks, Cleveland Cavaliers, and Indiana Pacers. But nothing was like the rivalry they had with the Detroit Pistons before the Bulls managed to climb to the top of the NBA ladder.

The Bulls and Pistons first met in the playoffs in spring 1989. But prior to that Jordan already had moments of tormenting the Bad Boys of Detroit. In March 1987, Jordan scored 61 points in a road overtime win to break the team record of 58 points he had set just a week earlier. It was his first 60-point regular-season effort.

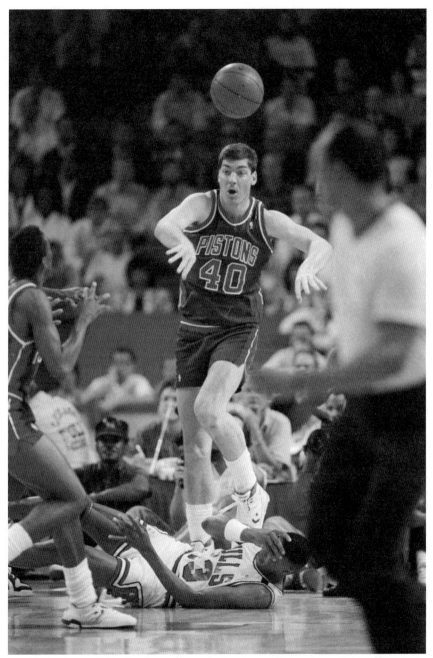

Scottie Pippen falls after being hit in the face by a Bill Laimbeer elbow in the 1989 playoffs.

In April 1988, he put 59 points on Detroit in a road win on Easter Sunday that helped propel the Bulls into the playoffs.

During the 1988–89 season, Detroit center Bill Laimbeer got into a fight that ended when Laimbeer threw Bulls coach Doug Collins over the scorer's table. Later that year, Isiah Thomas punched Bulls center Bill Cartwright, who had offended Thomas by standing in his way as Thomas entered the lane.

The previous season, the Pistons eliminated the Bulls from the playoffs in the second round, four games to one, winning both games that were played at Chicago Stadium. The Bulls were not able to solve the Pistons' physical style of play.

The Bulls once again made the playoffs in the '88–89 season, but this time they got through the first two rounds, beating Cleveland and New York to advance to the conference finals for the first time in the Jordan era. Again they were required to do battle with the Pistons.

The Pistons had beaten the Bulls in all six regular-season games. Oddly enough, the Bulls had the same 0–6 mark against Cleveland, but that did not matter as the Bulls topped the Cavaliers in the five-game, opening-round series.

Just as they had done in the Cleveland series, the Bulls took Game 1 as the road team against Detroit and won Game 3 at home to take a 2–1 lead in the best-of-seven series. But the Pistons won Game 4 at the Stadium and came up with a defensive plan that allowed Jordan only eight shots. The Pistons won the series 4–2, and a new rivalry was born.

In the 1989–90 season, the Bulls lost four of five regular-season games to the Pistons, but stretched the Pistons to seven games in the Eastern Conference Finals, only to lose again. It was thought that if the Bulls could earn home-court advantage in the series they would be able to win a Game 7.

By the time 1990–91 rolled around, the entire NBA was waiting for the rematch of the Bulls and Pistons in the Eastern

Conference Finals. The Pistons had won two straight NBA titles but knew the Bulls were aiming for them.

The Bulls had won the season series 3–2, and they had the youth and momentum going into the Finals, having won the division and conference top spot with 61 wins. But it turned out the Bulls did not need home-court advantage. They swept the Pistons in four games, and the final game featured one of the most ignoble moments in sports history, when Isiah Thomas led the Pistons starters off the floor with seconds to go in the game, walked past the Bulls bench and offered no congratulations to the new champions of the Eastern Conference.

The Pistons fell apart after that and the rivalry died as well. Oddly, former Piston Dennis Rodman—who once pushed Scottie Pippen into the basketball stanchion hard enough to give Pippen a lifelong scar on his face—went on to become a member of the Bulls in 1996, helping them to the final three championships of the dynasty years.

Hall of Fame

Michael Jordan was the first player in the Basketball Hall of Fame who played the most successful and significant years of his career with the Bulls. But there were other players who played for the Bulls and got to the Hall of Fame before Jordan.

Nate Thurmond, a center who made his name with the Golden State Warriors, played two seasons for the Bulls at the end of his career, from 1974–76. He was inducted into the Hall of Fame in 1985. The Ice Man, George Gervin, played most of his career with the San Antonio Spurs, but joined the Bulls for the 1985–86 campaign, during which Michael Jordan was injured, missing 64 games. Artis Gilmore, another center, played in the American Basketball Association before the NBA-ABA merger, and then joined the Bulls. He played six full seasons with the team from 1976–1982, then rejoined the Bulls for the end of his career in the 1987–88 season, during which he played in only 24 games. His best year with the Bulls was the 1978–79 campaign, when he averaged 23.7 points. Gilmore played all 82 games in five of the six seasons he was with the Bulls. He was inducted into the Hall of Fame in 2011. Robert Parish, yet another center, was inducted into the Basketball Hall of Fame in 2003 after a stellar career with the Boston Celtics. He spent 1996–97 with the Bulls as the third center behind Luc Longley and Bill Wennington. He had long been a favorite of Bulls general manager Jerry Krause.

Jordan was inducted into the Hall of Fame in 2009. He would have gone in sooner if he had not spent two seasons playing for the Washington Wizards after his Bulls career ended in 1998.

Jordan's Hall of Fame induction speech was one of the most memorable of all time, but not necessarily for a good reason. While most men accept their selection with humility, Jordan was blunt about the significance of his career and spoke about all the players who had great careers before him and how he eventually proved to be better than they were.

He even flew Leroy Smith, his former high school teammate, to the ceremony. Smith was the player that their high school coach chose to play on the varsity over Jordan when Jordan was just a sophomore. He seemed to make it clear that the decision might have been a mistake.

"He's still the same 6'7" guy, he's not any bigger, and his game is about the same," Jordan said. "But he started the whole process with me, because when he made the team and I didn't, I wanted to prove not just to Leroy Smith, not just to myself, but to the coach that picked Leroy over me, I wanted to make sure you understood—you made a mistake, dude."

The 2009 Hall of Fame Class included David Robinson of the San Antonio Spurs, former Bulls coach Jerry Sloan, John Stockton of the Utah Jazz, and women's basketball coach Vivian Stringer.

Scottie Pippen was inducted into the Basketball Hall of Fame in 2010 after spending 11 full seasons with the Bulls. He went on to play for Houston and Portland, then came back to the Bulls in 2003–04 to serve as an elder statesman.

Dennis Rodman was inducted into the Basketball Hall of Fame in 2011, after a career in which he played for (among others) the Detroit Pistons, San Antonio Spurs, and Bulls. He won five NBA titles and won the league's rebounding title an astonishing seven consecutive seasons. Rodman's induction gave the Bulls three inductees in three consecutive years: Jordan, Pippen, and Rodman.

The Bulls also have three coaches in the Hall of Fame. Sloan, who played for the Bulls and coached them for three seasons, also coached the Utah Jazz for two decades and was inducted into the Hall of Fame in 2009.

Phil Jackson was inducted into the Hall of Fame in 2007, even though he was still active as a coach. He coached the Bulls from 1989–1998 and won six titles. He then went on to win five more titles with the Los Angeles Lakers.

In 2011, longtime Bulls assistant coach and former college and NBA head coach Tex Winter was inducted into the Hall of Fame, with Chet "the Jet" Walker joining him in 2012.

60 2011—Vision of the Future

The summer of 2010 was a tumultuous one for the NBA. The stars were realigning. LeBron James was a free agent and a number of teams, including the Bulls, were jockeying for position to acquire him. Dwyane Wade was a free agent, as was Chris Bosh. The thinking was that a team would be able to acquire all three players and turn themselves into a superpower for many years to come.

The Bulls wanted to be that superpower, and they purged themselves of enough salary space that they could have acquired at least two of the three players and combine their skills with those of Derrick Rose to create a superteam, one that could bring multiple NBA titles to Chicago once again.

That team, however, ended up in Miami, where James, Wade, and Bosh combined for the 2010–11 season, creating an evil empire the league had not seen since the days of the Bad Boys Detroit Pistons.

The Bulls had all of that money to spend and signed free agent forward Carlos Boozer, guard-forward Kyle Korver, and guard Ronnie Brewer. They also picked up guard Keith Bogans to play with Rose, center Joakim Noah, and backup forward Taj Gibson.

They also got someone new to head this group. Coach Tom Thibodeau, who seemed as though he may end up a lifer as an assistant coach, was tabbed to work as the new head coach for the Bulls, replacing Vinny Del Negro, who'd been the coach for two struggling seasons.

Thibodeau introduced two concepts to the team instantly. He was going to use a starting lineup all season long, unless injury got in the way, and he was going to make sure the team played solid team defense to the greatest degree.

The NBA and its fan base were excited about the Bulls in 2010–11. They thought they might even have a slight chance of battling with the Miami Heat and the Boston Celtics for Eastern Conference supremacy.

The Bulls suffered setbacks throughout the season. Boozer sustained an injury in training camp and missed significant time at the beginning of the season. When he came back to action in December, Noah suffered an injury that took him out of action. The two interior talents played only about one quarter of the season together.

But the 2010–11 Bulls not only played defense better than any other team in the league, they had the deepest bench imaginable. In the absence of Boozer and Noah, veteran Kurt Thomas and Taj Gibson started or filled in significant minutes. Meanwhile, former Golden State starter C.J. Watson backed up Rose at the point, former Utah-starter Ronnie Brewer backed up veteran Bulls small forward Luol Deng, and former Utah forward Kyle Korver offered outside shooting that opened the game up for Rose and others in the middle.

Still, for much of the season, the Bulls trailed the Celtics and the Magic in the standings. The Heat, suffering under the pressure of intense expectations, had difficulty getting its collective act together until late in the season.

But in March and April, something happened that changed the course of the season.

One of the more remarkable aspects of the Bulls' season in 2010–11 was that they never lost more than two games in a row, matching the marks set by five of the six previous Bulls championship teams. (The first Bulls title team in 1990–91, the one that finally got over the Detroit hump and beat the Lakers in the final, started its season with three losses in a row.) From the All-Star break to the end of the regular season, the Bulls went 24–4. They won their last nine games.

Meanwhile, the Celtics were showing signs of age, and the Magic completely fell apart after a mid-season trade. The Heat were heating up, but by the time the regular season ended, the Bulls had the best record in the league at 62–20.

This exceeded expectations so greatly that some Bulls fans didn't know how to react. This kind of success had only been seen in Chicago more than a decade earlier, when the championship Bulls were going through their reign.

The Bulls battled past the Indiana Pacers and Atlanta Hawks in the first two rounds of the playoffs, setting up a much-anticipated matchup with the Heat in the Eastern Conference Finals.

With home-court advantage, the Bulls won Game 1 in decisive style, scoring a 103–82 victory that seemed to indicate their team-oriented approach and help defense would be able to deal with the Heat's star power. However, James, Wade, and Bosh, with the unexpected help from some bench players, negated the Bulls' advantages and won the next four games to take the series and advance to the NBA Finals. In the fifth and deciding game of the series, the Bulls let a 12-point lead disappear in the final three minutes, an indication that they perhaps were not yet ready to make the leap to the NBA Finals.

61 Jordan Scores 69

By the spring of 1990, Michael Jordan had already terrorized the good people of Cleveland on a couple of occasions. He led the Bulls to playoff victories over the Cavaliers in both '88 and '89, and the '89 series was won on Jordan's now-famous last-second shot over guard Craig Ehlo.

It was March of '90. The Bulls had advanced to the Eastern Conference Finals the year before and were aiming to get there again, looking for a rematch with the Detroit Pistons. They had left the Central Division rival Cavaliers behind in their dust over the previous couple of years.

On March 28, the Bulls had a game at Cleveland's Richfield Coliseum against the Cavaliers. The Bulls were closing in on a playoff spot. In the week before, Jordan had a pair of 40-plus-point games, but had scored "just" 28 in a home win against Phoenix on March 26.

But against the Cavaliers on March 28, Jordan scored 16 points in the first quarter, 15 points in the second quarter, then added 30 more points in the second half (with a game-high 20 in the third quarter). Still, the Cavaliers had forced overtime. Jordan scored eight more points in the extra period to finish with his career-high 69 points and the Bulls won 117–113.

In 50 minutes of action, Jordan made 23 of 37 shots, 21 of 23 free throws, and added 18 rebounds and six assists. Bulls coach Phil Jackson compared it to one of the greater performances he had ever seen out of scoring machine Pete Maravich back in the '70s.

Mark Price led the Cavaliers in scoring that night with 31 points.

At the time, Jordan's total was the ninth-highest single-game scoring total in NBA history. It was also the fourth 60-plus point game of his career. He only scored 60 one more time in his career, when he had 64 points in an overtime game against Orlando during the '92–93 season. He scored between 50 and 59 points 34 times.

The only other Bull in double figures in scoring the night Jordan scored 69 was Horace Grant, with 16. Bulls backup center Stacey King, always looking to make a joke, had one point that night and still says it was the night he and Michael Jordan combined for 70 points.

The Bulls were still traveling commercial at that point, and the Bulls stayed overnight in Cleveland before heading home to play the New York Knicks two nights later. So Jordan uncharacteristically joined some teammates and media members in the bar at the Cleveland Airport Marriott after the game. He was happy but extremely tired from his game performance that night.

Asked if he could ever score 100 points, Jordan shook his head. "I'm exhausted right now," Jordan said. "I can't imagine it."

For years after that game, the Bulls public relations staff ran the box score from that game in their annual media guide.

62 The Ray/Thurmond Trade

At the end of the 1974 season, when the Bulls lost to Kareem Abdul-Jabbar and the Milwaukee Bucks in the Western Conference Finals, coach Dick Motta decided the Bulls needed a stronger post presence. So he arranged a trade, sending Clifford Ray to the Golden State Warriors for veteran center Nate Thurmond.

The Bulls acquired Ray in the 1971 draft, and he played well enough as a rookie to make the league's All-Rookie team. But he and Tom Boerwinkle were no match for Wilt Chamberlain and Abdul-Jabbar, so Motta felt a change was needed.

Thurmond was 33 years old when he joined the Bulls, a veteran of 11 NBA seasons already. He started his Bulls career with an NBA-first quadruple-double: 22 points, 14 rebounds, 13 assists, and 12 blocked shots. But the Bulls were still a forward-led team, and Thurmond had trouble adjusting after being The Man at Golden State. Thurmond liked to score from the low post, and Motta did not run his offense through the low post.

Nate Thurmond averaged just 7.9 points and 11 rebounds per game for the Bulls in 1974–75.

Meanwhile, Clifford Ray was adjusting better to playing with the Warriors. He was only in his fourth year when he was traded, and had averaged 9.3 points and 12.2 rebounds in his last year with the Bulls. In 1975, though, Ray led the Warriors to the NBA championship. Although Rick Barry was the scoring star of that team, Ray led the team in rebounding and was second to only Barry in minutes played. More importantly, Ray led the Warriors over the Bulls' in the Western Conference Finals in what is often considered the Bulls best chance to reach the NBA Finals before the arrival of Michael Jordan.

That year, the Bulls were the best defensive team in the league, giving up just 95 points a game. Bob Love averaged 22 points per game, and Thurmond averaged 11 rebounds per contest.

After beating Kansas City-Omaha in the first round of the playoffs, the Bulls were pitted against the Warriors in the Western Conference Finals. The Warriors, with a 48–34 record, had home-court over the Bulls, who were 47–35 that season. But the Bulls took a 3–2 lead in the series with an upset win in Game 5 in Oakland.

In Game 6 at Chicago Stadium, the Bulls let a double-digit lead slip away behind the hot shooting of Barry. The Warriors won that game 86–72 to create the need for a Game 7 in Oakland.

Because the Bulls were a forward-driven team behind Bob Love and Chet Walker, Golden State coach Al Attles put Ray and George Johnson, the backup center, on those two forwards and the Bulls could not score late in the game. They gave up another double-digit lead and lost 83–79, allowing the Warriors to advance to the NBA Finals. There they swept the Washington Bullets for the 1975 title.

That was the end of an era for the Bulls. Chet Walker left the team, the '75–76 Bulls went 24–58, and Motta resigned at the end of the season to go to the Washington Bullets, where he won an NBA title.

63 Jordan as a Wizard

There was certainly something magical about what Michael Jordan did on the basketball court, but that doesn't mean anyone expected him to become a Wizard.

When Jordan retired from the Bulls the second time, after the 1998 season, he was almost 36 years old. He had won six NBA titles. He had fought the good fight back from his first retirement, the embarrassment of the '95 playoffs against Orlando when he looked old, and had proven himself again to be the greatest player of all time. He had sworn he would never play for a coach other than Phil Jackson, and said he would retire a Chicago Bull and not play for another team. He sat through a strike-shortened season, and both he and the league looked ready to move on to the next stage in their respective careers.

But Jordan's competitive spirit, and his need for the limelight, changed all that.

Jordan had always wanted to be involved with a team from an ownership standpoint, but it was a complicated issue with the Bulls, who had a solid ownership group led by Jerry Reinsdorf. Ownership possibilities seemed limited with the Bulls, so he became part owner and president of basketball operations for the Washington Wizards in January of 2000.

Jordan was in charge of the team's basketball operations, including draft picks and trades, a role in which he was only marginally successful.

In an attempt to spur the team, Jordan would occasionally practice with the club, showing that he had lost little of his athletic ability. So it came as no surprise in September of '01 when he announced he would return to active duty, this time with the Wizards.

In the '01–02 season Jordan played 60 games and averaged 22.9 points per game, with 5.2 assists. However, he suffered torn cartilage in his right knee, only the second significant injury of his career, the first being the broken foot he suffered in '85–86.

Sports Illustrated's Jack McCallum, one of the greatest NBA writers in league history, said Jordan would have been a first- or second-team All-NBA selection if he had played the entire season.

The Wizards led the NBA in home and road attendance in the '01–02 season until Jordan's injury. Jordan was the starting shooting guard for the Eastern Conference All-Star team that season, his 13th appearance overall and first as something other than a Chicago Bull.

Jordan came back healthy for the '02–03 season (during which he turned 40 years old) and played in all 82 games. He averaged 20 points per game, with 6.1 rebounds and 3.8 assists per game. He was again selected for the All-Star Game, but he was not voted in as a starter. Instead, he accepted an invitation from Vince Carter to take his starting spot, and he ended up playing 36 minutes and scoring 20 points.

Jordan could not personally will the Wizards to the postseason in '02–03, and he retired for a third time after the '03 campaign.

Jordan played his final game in April '03 in Philadelphia.

As an executive, Jordan proved to be a very good basketball player. In the '01 NBA draft, Jordan took high school talent

Kwame Brown with the No. 1 pick instead of Pau Gasol or Tyson Chandler, two players with far greater performances in the first decade of the new century. It was a selection that would dog Jordan through his days in Washington and into his following position with the Charlotte Bobcats.

In May '03, Jordan was fired as director of player personnel by Wizards owner Abe Pollin. Jordan has stated that he thought he had been used as a marketing ploy for the Wizards, saying he'd been hired only because the team thought he would play for them on the court.

64 The Jordan Rules

In 1988, Michael Jordan was still climbing the ladder of both basketball popularity and skill. He was still working to develop his outside shot. He preferred dunking the ball to anything else. He was still learning to trust his teammates. He was still without a title.

He did, however, have the ingredients for a title. Scottie Pippen and Horace Grant were on the team. John Paxson was with him. The Bulls were a year away from drafting key bench parts in Stacey King and B.J. Armstrong. In '89, Phil Jackson would replace Doug Collins as coach of the Bulls.

There was one thing standing in Jordan's way of getting a title. That one thing was the Detroit Pistons.

In '88, the Pistons beat the Bulls 4–1 in the Eastern Conference semifinals and won three of the four games by double digits. Jordan averaged 27 points per game against the Pistons, after averaging 45 against the Cleveland Cavaliers in the earlier round.

In '89, the Bulls advanced to the Eastern Conference Finals only to lose to the Pistons again, this time in six games. Jordan averaged almost 30 points per game that series, although he was held to 18 points in one game, in which he was also held to just eight shots from the field. The Bulls were unable to muster 100 points in any single game in the series, proof that the Jordan Rules were working.

Again in '90, the teams met in the Eastern Conference Finals. The series went the full seven games, and the Pistons had home-court advantage, which they used to record a 93–74 final-game victory. Jordan still averaged over 31 points per game in that series.

The Bulls finally got over the hump in '91, beating the Pistons in the Eastern Conference Finals on the way to their first NBA title.

So how did the Pistons keep Jordan and the Bulls down so long? They employed what became known as "The Jordan Rules."

The Jordan Rules were a variation on an old theme used against star players. Don't let one man beat you. Detroit coach Chuck Daly was determined to keep Jordan in check and let the rest of the Bulls players beat his team if they could.

The decision to play Jordan and the Bulls differently came after Jordan scored 59 points against the Pistons in a regular-season game at the end of the '88 season. The Bulls won by two points, and Daly had seen enough.

"We made up our minds right then and there that Michael Jordan was not going to beat us by himself again," Daly said.

The strategy was to play Jordan as physically as possible while changing the defensive strategy every time down the floor to keep Jordan thinking rather than playing. Coverage would change, challenges would come on the dribble up the floor one time, while Jordan stood with the ball on another, always with an element of physicality that earned the team the name "The Bad Boys." Jordan's every drive to the basket was met with something akin to brute force.

Jordan was also forced into the middle, where the Pistons' big men inside—Laimbeer, Mahorn, and Rodman—could help with the double- and triple-teams.

"It should be the easiest defense in the league to tear apart," Jordan said. "But we haven't done it."

In the '89 Eastern Conference playoffs, Daly decided to forego the Jordan Rules out of concern over what Scottie Pippen and Horace Grant could do against the Pistons inside if the Pistons did not spend enough defensive effort against the two forwards. But then Jordan scored 46 points in Game 3 of that series to give the Bulls a 2–1 edge, and the Pistons players asked Daly if they could reinstitute the Jordan Rules for the rest of the playoffs. They did, and the Pistons won the final three games of that series.

The system worked until Jordan and the Bulls fully adopted the Triangle Offense, which took advantage of defensive double-teams. Jordan had finally realized that Pippen, Grant, Paxson, and gawky center Bill Cartwright could score and could help him win. Any team that chose to spend its entire defensive effort to stop Jordan would find out that the other players on the team could contribute, especially if they were playing against a defense extended Jordan's way.

At the same time, the Pistons got old, suffering the pains of winning back-to-back NBA titles using a physical style that wears on a body, even when that body is the one inflicting the attack.

In a noticeable occurrence of history repeating itself, the Jordan Rules could have been renamed the Rose Rules for the way the Miami Heat manhandled Derrick Rose during the 2011 NBA Eastern Conference Finals. They sent double-teams at him from all directions, physically assaulted him on any drive to the lane, and waited for Rose's teammates to damage them. The damage never occurred.

65 Lucky Lottery Ball

Like most professional sports, the NBA has a draft of players coming out of high school or college who are eligible to play in the NBA. Like most professional sports, the NBA has a draft order based on performance. It used to be that the worst team from the previous season would get the first pick, the second worst the second pick, and on and on until the best team from the previous season made the final selection.

But by the time the 1980s had rolled around, however, it became a concern for the league that poor teams would lose games on purpose late in the season to give themselves a better spot in the upcoming talent draft. Late-season games became a joke, especially when they were played between two teams who were not going to qualify for the playoffs and were jockeying for a good draft spot.

So in '85 the NBA came up with the idea of a draft lottery. The idea was that the teams that did not make the playoffs each year would be placed in a lottery, and a selection of names would place those teams in a draft order. In that way the worst team in the league would not be guaranteed the No. 1 pick in the draft. It was meant to eliminate the rush to lose late in the season in order to garner the best spot in the draft.

For the first few years, each lottery team had an equal chance to be selected No. 1. Only the first three spots would be selected via the lottery; after that, the selections would go back to the order from the previous season's record.

In 1990, the NBA decided it wanted the worst teams to have the best chance to get a top lottery pick (sort of reversing field on the original reason for the lottery) and created a weighted system for the lottery. The worst team would be given the most chances at the No. 1 pick, without receiving an outright guarantee for that spot. The best team in the lottery (the best team not making the playoffs that year) would have a very small chance at the No. 1 pick.

The new system required the use of ping-pong balls, similar to the way most states run their legal-gambling lottery systems. A system is used where four of the 14 numbered balls are drawn, creating a four-digit combination. The lottery teams are assigned possible combinations by the NBA prior to the draft. The process is repeated for the second and third picks, then the rest of the draft order reverts to the teams with the worst records getting the top picks.

The entire process was mathematical and slightly confusing, but still managed to create situations where teams with very little mathematical chance at one of the top three spots somehow squeezed through.

In '93, the Orlando Magic got the No. 1 pick despite being the 11th-worst team in the league. They had a 1.5 percent chance of getting that pick.

In '99, the Bulls had the third-worst record in the league but got the No. 1 pick and selected Elton Brand out of Duke. Brand played two seasons with the Bulls, was the co-Rookie of the Year in '99–00 after averaging 20.1 points and 10 rebounds per game, but was traded by Bulls general manager Jerry Krause to the Los Angeles Clippers for the draft rights to Tyson Chandler. That move was generally regarded as a bust and led to Krause's eventual decision to resign. Brand was an All-Star for the Clippers in '02 and '06.

In '08, with a record of 33–49, the Bulls missed the playoffs for the first time in four years. They had the No. 9 pick in the draft, pre-lottery. According to the mathematical calculations from the draft, the Bulls had a 1.7 percent chance of getting the No. 1 pick.

But just as it had worked out for the Magic in '93, so it worked out for the Bulls in '08. In one of the great lottery upsets of all time, the Bulls got the No. 1 pick. After a month of deliberation, the Bulls selected Derrick Rose of Memphis rather than Michael Beasley of Kansas State with the first pick. Just as Brand did in '99–00, Rose won the league's Rookie of the Year award, and two years later Rose did Brand one better by being named the league's MVP.

Sometimes playing the lottery works out.

66 Rose or Beasley?

Today Derrick Rose is considered one of the best players ever to play for the Chicago Bulls, and considering the talent they've had, that's saying something. Rose's MVP award in the 2011 season was a testament to his athletic ability, his work ethic, and his humble nature in the face of great talent.

But when the Bulls selected Rose with the No. 1 pick in the '08 draft—a pick they were lucky to get thanks to the NBA draft lottery—they faced a dilemma that would change the fortunes of the team for years to come.

As the draft loomed in the summer of '08, there were two players considered to be the best available players in the draft. There was Rose, the point guard who had just completed his freshman year at the University of Memphis and had gone to the NCAA championship game, and Michael Beasley, Kansas State's first-team All-American power forward.

Beasley was the third-highest scorer in the nation in his freshman year at KSU. He led the nation in rebounding with more than

Commissioner David Stern congratulates Derrick Rose on being selected first overall by the Chicago Bulls in the 2008 NBA Draft.

12 per game. He was measured at 6'7" (shorter than his college "height" of 6'10"), but he was still considered a lock starter in the NBA. He was a low-post scoring threat, but there were character questions surrounding him.

Rose was a Chicago native who had won two state high school championships before going to Memphis. His character was unquestioned. But the Bulls were loaded at guard (as loaded as a bad team could be), with Ben Gordon, Kirk Hinrich, and Chris Duhon on the roster.

Back in '85, when the Bulls selected Michael Jordan with the third pick in the NBA draft, nobody knew how good he would be. Some might say they knew, but no one really knew. In similar fashion, there may be people who tell you Derrick Rose was a lock to be selected first by the Bulls in '08, but they would be lying.

The debate lasted from the May date when the Bulls got the No. 1 pick in the draft lottery to the late-June day when the draft was held. Do the Bulls select Beasley to offer inside help for guards Gordon and Hinrich, or do they load the backcourt with Rose, who could eventually force the Bulls to do something with one of their two talented starters?

The arguments went on forever. Sports radio could not stop debating the choice. Beasley was more talented, more athletically gifted. Rose was more of a competitor. The Bulls needed inside help. Gordon was already the scoring threat they needed on the outside.

An entire website was dedicated to the question, and Bulls general manager John Paxson was placed in the position of making the right choice.

Prior to the draft, a writer for *Sports Illustrated* wrote: "The obvious thought is to pick Chicago-native Derrick Rose. But Beasley is the most talented player in the draft, and the only thing the Bulls lack is an elite talent. For a franchise with championship aspirations, the early guess is that the Bulls risk passing up the sure thing in Rose to go for potentially the greatest thing in Beasley."

History tells us the Bulls selected Rose, who became the NBA's Rookie of the Year in 2009 and the MVP in 2011. The Miami Heat used the second pick of the 2008 draft to select Beasley, then traded him two years later to Minnesota.

It looks like Paxson got it right.

67 Jordan as a Charlotte Bobcat

In 1988, the NBA expanded into the Charlotte, North Carolina area. Long a hotbed of interest in college basketball, Charlotte was a burgeoning American city. The NBA conducted a series of tests involving demographics and business models and decided Charlotte would be a successful home for a professional basketball franchise.

It certainly helped that Michael Jordan had played collegiately at nearby University of North Carolina. Getting Jordan to return to the area twice a year seemed like a sure way to create a winning NBA market in the American southeast.

The Hornets were the first team located in Charlotte, and they remained in the city until 2002, when an ownership issue forced a move to New Orleans.

But the NBA was not interested in abandoning the city, so they gave Charlotte another expansion franchise. This time the Charlotte Bobcats arrived for the '04–05 season with a new ownership group.

In June '06, Jordan bought a minority ownership stake in the team, enough to be the second-largest shareholder in the club. Just as he was during his time with the Washington Wizards, Jordan was put in charge of all basketball operations, even though he had had little success in that role in the nation's capital.

In 2010, the Bobcats' primary owner was looking to sell, and Jordan had an ownership group looking to buy. In February '10 a deal was struck, and by March the NBA had approved the sale, making Jordan the first former player to be the majority owner of an NBA franchise.

Jordan holds friendship very dear, and he proved it with his hiring practices with the Bobcats. He removed Bernie Bickerstaff as coach and put former Bulls teammate Sam Vincent into the position. He hired his one-time best friend/teammate Rod Higgins to serve as general manager, hired former North Carolina guard Phil Ford as an assistant coach, and his former college roommate Buzz Peterson to serve as director of player personnel. Jordan had to fire Vincent after one season.

In the '09 draft, the Bobcats had the No. 12 selection and Jordan's team selected Gerald Henderson out of Duke University, the most hated college rival of Jordan's alma mater, North Carolina.

 # Jay Williams

From the time the Michael Jordan–led dynasty ended in 1998, the Bulls had several high draft picks, in part because they had such poor records on the floor. They lucked into the No. 1 pick in '99 and selected Elton Brand of Duke, and in '02 they got the No. 2 pick and selected another Dukie, 6'2" guard Jay Williams. They actually had the highest probability of getting the No. 1 pick in '02 (tied with Golden State for worst record the previous season), and would have had a shot at Chinese superstar Yao Ming, but

Houston got the first selection in the draft lottery and the Bulls fell to No. 2.

By this point, the Bulls had reinvented themselves, rebuilding their interior with the deals that got them Tyson Chandler and Eddy Curry (and made them give up Brand). Their backcourt was talented but flighty: former Fab Five guard Jalen Rose from Michigan and sharp-shooting but mercurial Jamal Crawford.

With the second pick in the draft, the Bulls went back to Duke, one of the most successful college basketball programs in America, to select Williams. It turned out to be a decent selection; the only true superstar selected after Williams that year was high schooler Amare Stoudemire, and the Bulls were already loaded with high schoolers turned into pros with Chandler and Curry.

At Duke, Williams was ACC Rookie of the Year, averaging 14.5 points his freshman year. As a sophomore, he led the Blue Devils to the NCAA Championship and averaged 21.6 points per game to lead the ACC in scoring. In '02, as one of the nation's best three-point shooters and as talented as a passer as he was a scorer, he was named the College Basketball Player of the Year.

After he was drafted, he played for the United States in the '02 FIBA World Championship. That team was knocked out of the Indianapolis-based tournament in the quarterfinals by Yugoslavia.

Still, Williams came to the Bulls with a reputation both as a winner, a scorer, and a passer. With former Bulls center Bill Cartwright as his coach, he started most of his first year as a pro, battling Crawford for playing time the entire year. He finished with 9.5 points per game and almost five assists per game. In only his seventh game of the season, against the New Jersey Nets, he had his best game as a pro with 26 points, 14 rebounds, and 13 assists.

Then tragedy struck.

On June 19, 2003, just before the '03 NBA draft, as the Bulls were making plans to build on the 30–52 team from the previous

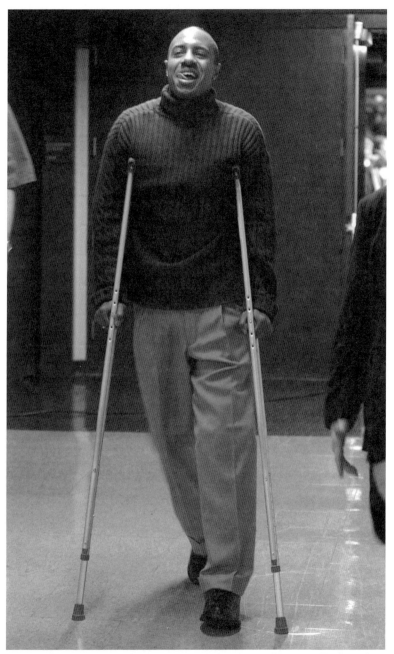

Roughly six months after his motorcycle accident, Jay Williams walks through the United Center.

season, Williams crashed his motorcycle into a Chicago streetlight. He was not wearing a helmet and was not licensed to drive a motorcycle in Illinois. He suffered a severed main nerve in his leg, fractured his pelvis, and tore three ligaments in his left knee. His basketball career was over. He never played another game for the Bulls, nor did he ever return to action in the NBA.

Making matters worse, he violated his contract by driving a motorcycle. Still, the Bulls did the noble thing, paying him $3 million in a contract buyout even though they did not legally have to pay him a single cent of his rookie contract thereafter.

Because of the injury, the Bulls drafted Kansas swing guard Kirk Hinrich out of necessity.

Williams attempted a comeback, and got into good enough shape that the New Jersey Nets signed him to a contract in '06, three years after the motorcycle accident. He was waived before that season began, however.

Williams eventually earned a position with ESPN as a commentator for high school and college basketball broadcasts.

69 Bulls in Paris

In the late 20th century, the NBA began to expand its brand into the rest of the world. Europe was suddenly a hotbed of basketball activity, with the exposure of the Yugoslavian national team and reports that Italy was sponsoring excellent club basketball. The NBA wanted to get a piece of the action across the pond.

While there was talk of an NBA franchise opening in London, the NBA made its first official foray into Europe when it agreed to participate in the McDonald's Championship, an eight-team competition between an NBA team and seven club teams from leagues throughout Europe.

The competition was always won by the NBA representative. In 1987, it was the Milwaukee Bucks, followed by the Boston Celtics ('88), Denver Nuggets ('89), New York Knicks ('90), Los Angeles Lakers ('91), and Phoenix Suns ('93).

By '95, in an attempt to legitimize the competition a bit more, the NBA agreed to send its reigning champion. The Houston Rockets went to London in '95, and in '97 the Chicago Bulls represented the league in Paris.

The team was really not excited about going to Paris. After all, they had just completed their second consecutive world championship and were gearing up for what seemed likely to be the last season for Michael Jordan, Scottie Pippen, and Phil Jackson to be together.

Although Michael Jordan had traveled the world to play golf or to represent the interests of Nike, the sportswear and equipment giant he worked for, he had never been to Paris. He was uncertain whether he wanted to get started again for the next season with an exhibition tournament on a world stage at Paris' Palais Omnisports de Bercy.

Another problem with the trip is that Jordan was going alone, in a manner of speaking. His star sidekick Scottie Pippen stayed home recovering from foot surgery, and star weirdo Dennis Rodman stayed home in a contract dispute.

The Bulls did have Toni Kukoc, who was a star in Italy for a number of years before agreeing to join the Bulls. Oddly, Kukoc's former team, Benetton Treviso, was one of the teams invited to the tournament.

And the Bulls also had Phil Jackson, who was a Montana-born and bred American who had a European flair about him.

The Bulls defeated Paris-St. Germain and Olympiakos of Greece, which had won the previous year's European club championship. The title game was won 104–78.

The Bulls were in Paris for about four days, but the whirlwind visit proved not only that the NBA had the best basketball product in the world, but that the Bulls could command the world's attention, not just a nation's attention.

The last McDonald's Championship was played in '99. The San Antonio Spurs won the tournament played in Milan.

70 Jordan the Actor

Michael Jordan has a presence on the small screen that seemed immeasurable. His good looks and quick smile, with his ability to speak clearly and deliver his lines with a sense of reality, made him a favorite for product endorsements. He was always a natural.

It seemed inevitable that Jordan would cross over into filmmaking, but he wasn't a good enough actor to deliver a performance outside of his area of expertise. Finally, though, he agreed to do a film for Warner Brothers called *Space Jam*, in which he appeared alongside animated legends Bugs Bunny, Elmer Fudd, Marvin the Martian, and the rest of the Warner Brothers' cartoon catalog.

The plot of the movie involved basketball, and Jordan brought along some of the more famous players in the NBA at the time, including one of his best friends, Charles Barkley, as well as Patrick Ewing, Larry Johnson, Muggsy Bogues, and Shawn Bradley. Also in the movie were basketball legend Larry Bird and

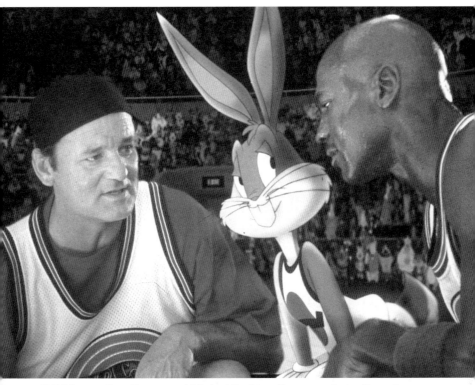

Bill Murray, Bugs Bunny, and Michael Jordan talk strategy during Space Jam.

Bill Murray, considered one of the most famous actors to come out of Chicago.

Jordan's best moment in the film, outside of the many shots of him playing basketball in a decisive plot-driven game, is when Bugs Bunny kisses him.

The film grossed $230 million worldwide and remains a very popular rental film for kids and Bulls fans.

Jordan made the film in '95 for a '96 release. The storyline followed his true life, in which he was a retired basketball player pursuing a career in baseball. He is drawn back to the basketball floor to help the Looney Tunes win a basketball game against other animated characters. When he wins the basketball game by himself with a hyper-extended version of one of his signature free throw line dunks, he realizes he wants to return to basketball. The storyline mirrored his own return to basketball in the spring of '95 after a short retirement.

In '91, after the Bulls won their first championship, Jordan fever was at a new peak. *Saturday Night Live*, the iconic late-night program that filmed in New York but had a great connection with Chicago, invited Jordan to host the season opener. In the 16 previous seasons of *SNL*, only a few athletes had been asked to host, including football stars Joe Montana and Walter Payton. In season five, former Boston Celtics star Bill Russell hosted the show.

Aired on September 28, 1991, Jordan's appearance was met with great approval. One of his best moments came in a skit with the character Stuart Smalley, played by comedian Al Franken, who eventually became a U.S. Senator from Minnesota. Smalley was a character who was not a therapist but tried to help people get through their emotional and psychological crises, and in order to help Jordan (playing himself), Smalley had him look into a mirror and say "I'm good enough, I'm smart enough, and doggone it, people like me." Considering Jordan's brimming personal self-confidence, it was a very funny skit.

He also starred in a skit with the Superfans, a regular comedic skit of mustachioed Chicago fans who venerated Ditka and the Bears as gods. After the Bulls won the title in '91, the Superfans became Bulls fans, and in the *SNL* skit, Jordan was required to wear a hula skirt and dance.

Chet Walker

The Bulls surprised the NBA with 33 wins in their expansion campaign, but failed to grow after that. In the 1968–69 season, the Bulls missed the playoffs for the first time, and second-year coach Dick Motta was anxious to put together a winner.

On September 2, 1969, the Bulls traded forward Jim Washington and future considerations to the Philadelphia 76ers for forward Chet "The Jet" Walker and Shaler Halimon. It was considered a steal of a deal for the Bulls, who were getting a star forward from the championship 76ers for a player far below his abilities.

Walker was already an established star when he joined the Bulls. He played on the '66–67 NBA champion 76ers, which won a league-record 68 games that season. He averaged 19.3 points per game that season and shot almost 49 percent from the field. By the time the Bulls acquired him, he had already been an NBA All-Star three times with Philadelphia.

He also had Illinois connections. He played his college basketball at Bradley University in Peoria. During his time there, the Braves twice won the National Invitation Tournament (a tournament that competed with the NCAA tournament for teams).

He was selected 14th overall in the 1962 NBA draft by the Syracuse Nationals, who became the Philadelphia 76ers after the '62–63 season. Walker scored 12.3 points his rookie season to make the NBA's All-Rookie team. In his second season as a pro he averaged 17.3 points and 10.3 rebounds and made the NBA's Eastern Conference All-Star team.

Walker was the final ingredient in creating a roster that propelled the Bulls to the highest level the team achieved in its first

Maurice Lucas Was/Was Not a Bull?

In 1974, coming off three consecutive 50-plus-win seasons, the Bulls found themselves with an opportunity to improve themselves further in the collegiate draft. They selected power forward Maurice Lucas out of Marquette with the 14th-overall pick and small forward Cliff Pondexter out of Long Beach State with the 16th pick. Their jobs were going to be to back up Bob Love and Chet Walker until those two got old and the youngsters were ready.

But Bulls owner Arthur Wirtz, a notorious negotiator and certainly not a basketball mind, told the staff they could only sign one of the two rookies. Coach Ed Badger made the choice to go after Pondexter, who was proving to be an easier target to sign than Lucas, who fired one agent before he even began negotiating with the Bulls.

Pondexter played three seasons for the Bulls and never averaged more than 5.8 points per game. Lucas went on to be a perennial All-Star, redefined the position of power forward with his strength and interior defense, and won an NBA title with Portland.

decade. He joined with Bob Love, Jerry Sloan, Tom Boerwinkle, and Norm Van Lier to create the finest Bulls team ever, until Michael Jordan came along, that is.

But he did not make the move willingly. After growing up poor in Benton Harbor, Michigan, he had made his home in Philadelphia and wanted to stay. He reportedly considered retirement before agreeing to join the Bulls.

Walker played six seasons for the Bulls, averaged over 20 points per game the first three years and averaged 19 points per game the last three. He led the league in free throw percentage one year and made the Western Conference All-Star team four more times as a Bull, for a total of seven All-Star appearances.

Walker, a 6'7" power forward, was best known for his one-on-one moves. His pump fake was legendary, producing either a shot or a trip to the free throw line as defenders failed to know for sure when he was going to shoot. With all the other talent the Bulls had for those successful years, Walker was the best clutch shooter.

Walker was the definition of a winner. During his six seasons with the Bulls, the team had four consecutive 50-win seasons and never had a losing campaign.

In the summer of '75, Walker asked for a new contract, estimated at $200,000 a year. The team refused to give him a new contract and also refused to trade him. Walker was already 35 years old and suffering from tendonitis in his knees, so he retired from the game.

After retiring, Walker got involved in filmmaking, and eventually earned an Emmy Award as co-producer of a made-for-TV movie titled *A Mother's Courage*, the story of the life of the mother of former star NBA guard Isiah Thomas. He was inducted into the Basketball Hall of Fame in 2012.

72 Post-Dynasty Years

Phil Jackson had tired of coaching the Chicago Bulls and dealing with general manager Jerry Krause. He was ready to move on to new challenges.

Krause was ready to pull another Svengali. He felt he was responsible for bringing Jackson into NBA head coaching, felt Jackson was not appreciative enough, and wanted to prove he could find another Jackson somewhere.

The first other Jackson was Tim Floyd, who was a college coach at Iowa State whom Krause had met through recruiting. The two men shared a love of fishing, and Krause wanted to reward his new fishing buddy by bringing him up to the NBA.

But Floyd could not succeed with the talent Krause gave him.

The post-dynasty breakup included Michael Jordan's retirement, Scottie Pippen's trade to Houston, Luc Longley's trade to Phoenix, and Steve Kerr's trade to San Antonio. Dennis Rodman was not re-signed. The only key players left from the three title teams from '96–98 were Toni Kukoc, Ron Harper, and Bill Wennington.

The disagreement over a new collective bargaining agreement forced the league to cancel games until February. In the shortened season, the Bulls went 13–37. Kukoc was the only real scoring threat, averaging 18.8 points per game. Harper had to contribute 11 points per game just to keep the Bulls close.

In 1999–00, with rookie sensation Elton Brand and trouble-making swingman Ron Artest (Harper and Wennington were gone and Kukoc was traded midway through the season), the Bulls went 17–65. Brand averaged 20 points per game and was co-Rookie of the Year.

In 2000–01, with yet another collection of tagalong players surrounding Brand, the Bulls went 15–67 and had the longest losing streak in team history with 16 straight losses.

In the summer of 2001, Krause had what he thought was going to be his biggest draft day success since getting Scottie Pippen and Horace Grant in 1987. He drafted Chicago high school center Eddy Curry and got Los Angeles high-schooler Tyson Chandler from the Clippers for Brand, who had not only been the NBA Rookie of the Year two years prior, but was considered one of the league's best up-and-coming low-post scoring and rebounding threats.

But the Bulls went 4–21 through the first 25 games and Floyd resigned on Christmas Day 2001.

Former Bulls center Bill Cartwright was already on the team as an assistant coach and he had always been a favorite of Krause's because he was one of the few players who never spoke badly of him. So Krause elevated him to head coach on December 28, 2001. The Bulls finished 21–61.

In 2002–2003, with Cartwright at the helm, the Bulls went 30–52. The Chandler-Curry thing was not working out, and the Bulls had no quality outside scoring threats.

In the summer of 2003, now five years removed from the championship years and with no salvation in sight, Krause resigned. Former Bulls player, assistant coach, and broadcaster John Paxson was hired to take his place, and one of the first things Paxson had to do was fire his former teammate Cartwright as coach.

Paxson started to rebuild, beginning with the hiring of former player and coach Scott Skiles, a no-nonsense guy who spoke Paxson's language. Paxson acquired Kirk Hinrich, Luol Deng, Ben Gordon, and Andres Nocioni, and things began to look up again for the club.

First Winning Team

Over the first few years, the Bulls had acquired the kind of talent that made a decent team. By 1970, future Hall of Famer Jerry Sloan was still with the team, former first-round pick Tom Boerwinkle was handling the middle, proving to be one of the best passing centers in the league, and in November of '68, during coach Dick Motta's first season, the Bulls traded Flynn Robinson to Milwaukee for forward Bob Love and guard Bobby Weiss. They acquired forward Chet Walker from Philadelphia in '69, and suddenly the Bulls looked like a real team.

The trade for Love and Weiss was considered a horrible deal for the Bulls, who twice tried to get rid of Love immediately after getting him. Instead, they ended up with a player who would play nine seasons for the team, lead the team in scoring for seven seasons, make the All-Star team three times, and get his jersey No. 10 retired in 1994.

The roster also included guard Matt Guokas, picked up from Philadelphia, and guard Jimmy Collins.

This was the first signature team for the Bulls. The starting lineup of Love, Walker, Boerwinkle, Sloan, and Weiss played together for a number of years and had the team's first real success.

The '70–71 season was the first in which the NBA broke its teams up into divisions. There were 17 teams total, and they were split into four divisions, two in the Western Conference and two in the Eastern Conference. The Bulls were in the Midwest Division with Detroit, Milwaukee, and Phoenix. Playoff spots were given to the first two teams in each division.

The Bulls won five of their first seven games and remained above .500 the rest of the season. They had a six-game winning streak in December, and in February they went 11–3 to establish themselves in the playoff race.

In March, against the rival Milwaukee Bucks, the Bulls won 110–103 in overtime when Boerwinkle grabbed 33 rebounds, a one-game team record that still stands. He outplayed future Hall of Famer Lew Alcindor (who became Kareem Abdul-Jabbar later in his career). That also ended the Bucks' 20-game winning streak, which was the longest in league history at the time.

The Bucks won the NBA title that year, winning 66 games in the regular season.

The Bulls ended up going 51–31, the team's first winning team and obviously its first 50-win season. The Bulls ended up as the second-best defensive team in the league, holding opponents to 105.4 points per game (in a far more offensive world than today's game).

Motta was named NBA Coach of the Year, the second such award for the Bulls franchise in its five years of existence (Johnny "Red" Kerr won the award in the team's initial season). Love was named to the West All-Star team. Love set the team record for points with 2,043 in the season.

The Bulls extended the Lakers to seven games in the first round of the playoffs before being eliminated.

Year Number Two

The Chicago Bulls entered their second season with an impressive new forward, Clem Haskins, who'd played at Western Kentucky. Erwin Mueller had moved into the starting lineup in his second year, and Barry Clemens was now the starting forward with Bob Boozer. Guy Rodgers was the starting point guard for the first game, but soon thereafter was traded to Cincinnati for Flynn Robinson, cash, and two draft choices in late October. The Bulls had lost forward Don Kojis to the San Diego Rockets in the league's expansion draft.

The trade of Rodgers was one of the team's first silly mistakes. Rodgers was the team's leading scorer at 18.0 points per game in the first season and had led the league in assists with 11.2 per game. He was a star for a fledgling team and he was sent away in what was essentially a money-and-picks deal.

The Bulls were also playing without a true center. Erwin Mueller, by most standards a classic power forward, was playing the middle, but at 6'8" was dwarfed by many of his matchup centers.

In January '67, while the Bulls were playing their home games at the Chicago Amphitheatre in their first NBA season, the huge exhibition hall McCormick Place, located on the coast of Lake Michigan, suffered a massive fire, and the city's active convention business was set to suffer. Instead, much of the city's business was transferred to the Amphitheatre, and the Bulls were forced to move to the Chicago Stadium, the "Old Barn" on the west side, which was home to the Chicago Blackhawks, the far more established NHL team. The Stadium seated 18,000 for basketball, more than double the capacity of the Amphitheatre, and the Bulls were worried their small crowd would get lost in the building.

The Bulls started their second season by losing their first nine games and 15 of their first 16. The slow start prompted owner Dick Klein to trade Rodgers to Cincinnati for Robinson, the money, and the draft choices. Robinson was more of a shooter than a floor general, and the Bulls had to slow their game up.

Mueller played only 35 games for the Bulls that season. He spent part of the season playing for the upstart American Basketball Association.

Boozer made the West All-Star team, and despite a record of 29–53, the Bulls again made the playoffs in the West (the league expanded again that season into San Diego and Seattle, and their presence in the Western Conference made it easier to get into the playoffs). They finally won a game in the postseason thanks to a 41-point game by Robinson, but were eliminated 4–1 by the Los Angeles Lakers. Boozer led the team in scoring with 21.5 points.

At season's end, Jerry Colangelo, who was instrumental in getting the team started, left to run the new Phoenix Suns expansion club, and he took coach Johnny "Red" Kerr with him. The

Bulls named Dick Motta, who was coaching at Weber State in Idaho, as his successor.

In the '68 draft, the Bulls selected center Tom Boerwinkle out of the University of Tennessee with the No. 4 pick. He played for the Bulls for 10 seasons and remained the No. 2 rebounder in total boards for the Bulls into the 21st century.

Horace Grant

When the Bulls were on their way to their first three-peat of championships, there was a pecking order of fame. It started with Michael Jordan. Scottie Pippen grew into the No. 2 star. Coach Phil Jackson was well on his way to superstardom as well.

Horace Grant was the fourth wheel on the team, and it did not always sit well with him. But the Bulls would not have been as good as they were without his contributions inside.

Horace Grant was born, along with his identical twin brother Harvey, in Georgia, and became a talented collegiate basketball player at Clemson. (Harvey played at Oklahoma after one year at Clemson.) Horace Grant was drafted by the Bulls in 1987, 10th overall, in the dramatic selection day that also brought Pippen to the Bulls with the fifth pick. (Pippen was selected by Seattle but traded to the Bulls in a pre-draft agreement.) Finding Pippen and Grant on the same day was the crowning achievement of the career of general manager Jerry Krause.

When Grant was chosen, there was another collegiate power forward-type available. Joe Wolf of North Carolina was still on the board, and Michael Jordan would have liked nothing better than to have another Tar Heel on the team. The selection of Grant instead of Wolf did not sit well with Jordan.

Grant first played behind forward Charles Oakley, a well-known and popular rebounding specialist. When Oakley was traded to the Knicks for Bill Cartwright in the summer of '88, Grant moved into the starting lineup. He was the Bulls' leading rebounder in his second NBA season and remained so for the next five seasons, averaging almost 10 rebounds per game in the '91–92 season.

Grant, nicknamed "The General" after General Ulysses S. Grant, was best known for his defense, but he was the third scoring option for the Bulls through much of their championship run from '91–93. With Jordan on the team, Grant's scoring average grew to 14.2 in '92, and in the year after Jordan retired he averaged a career-high 15.1.

Grant was named to the NBA All-Defensive team four times and made the All-Star team in '94, when Michael Jordan had retired and Grant became the No. 2 option on a good but not great Bulls team.

But Grant always felt slighted by the light of fame that shone so brightly on Jordan and Pippen. Although he and Pippen often described themselves as brothers through their early career, Grant grew unhappy as Pippen was named to the Olympic squad in '92.

After Jordan and Pippen played in the Dream Team Olympics in '92, Bulls coach Phil Jackson gave the two star players preferential treatment in training camp, telling them to take it easy since he knew they were already in shape. Grant saw that as yet another example of the double standard evident in the Bulls' locker room and was not shy about complaining about it.

The Bulls played the New York Knicks in the conference finals in '93, and the Knicks had home-court advantage after winning 60 games to the Bulls' 57 in the regular season. In Game 5 of the series, which was tied at 2–2, Grant was responsible for keeping New York's Charles Smith from scoring on several put-back attempts in the game's final seconds, and the Bulls won that game and the next to advance to the NBA finals for the third year in a row.

In the '93 NBA Finals, the Bulls led the series 3–2 heading into Game 6 in Phoenix. With the Bulls trailing by two points late in the game, Scottie Pippen drove the lane and passed the ball deep inside to Grant, who quickly turned out rather than shoot and saw John Paxson on the left side at the three-point line. Paxson made the basket that won the game 99–98. The Suns still had a couple of seconds to try to get the game-winner, but Grant blocked a shot in the lane by Phoenix's Kevin Johnson in the final second to preserve the win and the title for the Bulls.

After winning three titles with Chicago, he left the team as a free agent in the summer of '94. He played for Orlando, Seattle, and the Lakers, where he reunited with coach Phil Jackson. Grant won a fourth NBA title with the Lakers in '01.

As a member of the Magic in '95, Grant averaged 18 points and shot almost 65 percent from the field as the Magic beat the Bulls in the second round of the playoffs. That was the year Jordan came back in March from his first retirement, was clearly out of shape, and the Magic took advantage of that. That loss prompted Jordan to rededicate himself over that summer, leading to three more titles from '96–98.

Harvey Grant, Horace's twin brother, played at Oklahoma collegiately, then played for several teams in the NBA but never had the success Horace did.

76 The Duke Connection

The greatest player in Bulls history, Michael Jordan, played collegiately at the University of North Carolina. The Tar Heels' most hated rival are the Blue Devils of Duke University. That did not stop Jordan from begging the Bulls to acquire former Duke star Johnny Dawkins in the 1986 NBA draft. The Bulls took Brad Sellers of Ohio State instead, and Jordan gave Sellers a very hard time while the two were together as members of the same team. That decision actually started a difficult relationship between Jordan and Bulls general manager Jerry Krause over player acquisitions.

The first Duke star player selected by the Bulls in the NBA draft was Tate Armstrong back in '77, before Jordan became a Bull and Chicago cared about the North Carolina Tar Heels. Armstrong did not pan out, playing just two seasons with the team.

In '85, the Bulls traded with San Antonio for veteran forward Gene Banks, another Dukie. Banks played for the team for two years.

The Bulls did not try again with Duke until they got the No. 1 pick in the '99 draft and selected interior-stud Elton Brand, who earned Rookie of the Year honors in '00 and remained in the NBA well into the next decade.

In '02, the Bulls had the No. 2 pick in the draft and selected guard Jay Williams out of Duke. Williams played well for the Bulls for one season before injuring himself right out of basketball in a motorcycle accident in the city of Chicago in the summer of '03.

In '04, the Bulls waited until the second round to get Duke guard Chris Duhon, who played well for the Bulls for four seasons before getting pushed out of the player rotation by Ben Gordon and Kirk Hinrich.

Also in June '04, the Bulls acquired the rights to Duke small forward Luol Deng from Phoenix in exchange for a series of draft picks. As of 2012, Deng has completed eight seasons with the team. He was one of the most dependable players on the team that advanced to the Eastern Conference Finals in 2011 and made his first All-Star team in 2012.

In the summer of 2010, the NBA rosters turned on their heads as superstars LeBron James, Dwyane Wade, and Chris Bosh were all available as free agents. The three of them decided to play together in Miami, but the Bulls, who had tried to attract all three of them but failed, got the next best player available for the '10–11 season in former Duke and Utah Jazz forward Carlos Boozer, who preceded Deng at Duke.

Oddly, after selecting Jordan in '84, the Bulls did not pick another North Carolina player until '98, when they selected Shammond Williams in the second round of the draft. Williams never played for the Bulls.

In '90, the Bulls did sign rookie free agent Scott Williams, a forward out of North Carolina. Williams played four seasons for the Bulls and was a key reserve on the first three championship teams.

77 Rodman the Actor and Entertainer

Michael Jordan and Dennis Rodman were so extremely different. Jordan was the consummate professional athlete, had a good relationship with the media, was respectful of others, and was

Rodman arrives at the world premier of Double Team *in 1997.*

employed as a role model by parents. Rodman was a freak, a multi-tattooed, crazy-haired basketball lunatic who was always ready to get into trouble, ran afoul of basketball officials and the law, and was considered the worst-possible role model ever.

But Jordan and Rodman had something in common. They were both multimedia stars. Jordan was a favorite for television commercials; Rodman was a favorite for athletic sideshows.

After the Bulls dynasty broke up in 1998, Rodman continued to play basketball. He played a few games for the Lakers in '98–99 and played 12 games for the Mavericks in '99–00. He played for many minor league teams for several years after that, always hoping some NBA team would give him a call-up for a late-playoff run. It never materialized.

Rodman also experimented with a career in TV and movies. In '96, while he was playing his first season with the Bulls, he had a reality TV show on MTV called *The Rodman World Tour*, in which he interviewed stars. It included one episode when he conducted the interviews from bed.

In '97, during the off-season, he made his first foray into serious filmmaking with an action adventure movie called *Double Team*, in which he played the hero alongside famed action star Jean-Claude Van Damme. The two teamed up for another action film titled *Simon Sez* in '99. Rodman also appeared in a relatively successful film titled *The Comebacks* in '07, playing against type as a prison warden.

In '98, he won three Razzie awards (given for bad acting, sort of the inverse to the Oscars) for Worst New Star, Worst Screen Couple, and Worst Supporting Actor. In '00, he was nominated, but did not win, for Worst New Star of the Decade.

He also had a starring role in a short-lived TV series titled *Special Ops Forces*, in which he played a special military operations expert.

He appeared on a television show titled *Celebrity Mole*, in which small-time celebrities competed against each other with one of the stars acting as a "mole" for the show's producers. He won the contest.

On two occasions, once on television and once in a movie, it was suggested Rodman might be an alien. He made an appearance on the TV show *Third Rock From the Sun* as himself, but it was made clear that he was actually from outer space. In the movie *Men in Black*, the final scene carried a line that stated that Rodman was an alien.

Like Jordan, Rodman made an appearance on *Saturday Night Live*, but his was a short cameo appearance.

Rodman also made a couple of forays into professional wrestling, which appeared to be a perfect fit for him. He teamed with world-famous wrestler Hulk Hogan at two *Bash at the Beach* wrestling events.

78 Joakim Noah

In the summer of 2007, the Chicago Bulls were in yet another transition period. With Kirk Hinrich, Luol Deng, and Ben Gordon on the roster, they were young and athletic in the backcourt and from the outside, but needed strength on the inside. They needed someone who could grab a key rebound, someone who could draw attention away from the backcourt players and create some havoc in the paint.

They didn't know they needed personality, too, but that's what they got.

The '07 NBA draft was not considered deep in interior talent once you got past Greg Oden of Ohio State, who was the No. 1-overall pick by the Portland Trail Blazers.

But there was one unique aspect to the draft that year. The University of Florida Gators had won back-to-back national championships at the college level, and three of the players from those teams were jumping to the NBA. They were forward-center Al Horford, guard Corey Brewer, and center Joakim Noah.

The Bulls were coming off an exciting season in which they went 49–33 and advanced to the second round of the playoffs. They swept the defending champion Miami Heat in the first round and lost to the Detroit Pistons in the second round in a hard-fought series. They were looking to move up.

Although they made the playoffs, they owned the first round pick of the New York Knicks from an earlier move, and the Knicks were in the draft lottery. The Knicks/Bulls ended up with the No. 9 pick.

From the Florida group, Horford went No. 3 to the Atlanta Hawks and Brewer went No. 7 to the Minnesota Timberwolves. The Bulls selected Noah at No. 9. The trio became the highest drafted three players from the same school in NBA history.

Noah was 6'11", with unique passing skills from the center position, and an emotional side that was both a concern and an attractive aspect for the Bulls.

While Hinrich had the ability to be a bit of a firebrand, Deng and Gordon were unemotional in their approach to the game. Noah, a showman and a counterculture personality, as well as a warm, caring individual who brought a true passion onto the floor, was going to serve as a counterpoint to the passionless state of the Bulls in the mid-decade.

In college, Noah was a scorer. He led the Gators in scoring his sophomore year with 14 points a game. In the '06 NCAA tournament, he scored 26 points with 15 rebounds in a regional final against top-ranked Villanova. In the final game against UCLA he had 16 points, nine rebounds, and an NCAA championship game record six blocked shots.

It was believed that he would have been one of the top players selected in the '06 draft as a sophomore, but he stayed at Florida for a shot at a title repeat, and got it in '07.

Born of famous parents, French tennis star Yannick Noah and Swedish beauty Cecilia Rodhe, Noah was well-prepared for the glamour of the NBA. His paternal grandfather, Zacharie Noah, was a professional soccer player from Cameroon.

Noah displayed his unique personality on draft day when he showed up in a pinstriped cream prom suit, with a bow tie, his

Joakim Noah greets the world at the 2007 NBA Draft.

long, curly hair squirting out from under the Bulls hat he was given upon his selection. He looked like a kid having a very good time.

It took a while for Bulls fans to figure out what they had in Noah. He averaged 6-plus points per game in both of his first two seasons, with 5.6 rebounds in his first season and 7.6 rebounds in his second. His spirit was undeniable, but it wasn't clear how his spirit would transfer to wins. The Bulls went 33–49 in his first season, and coach Scott Skiles was fired at Christmas. In the first season under new coach Vinny Del Negro, the '08–09 season, the Bulls pulled up to 41–41 and made the playoffs.

However, in the '09 playoffs, at the end of his second season, Noah made a name for himself with a strong performance in the first-round series against the Boston Celtics, the overwhelming favorite to win the Eastern Conference title. Noah averaged 10 points and 13 rebounds in that series, and in the third overtime of Game 6, Noah made a huge steal near midcourt, dribbled down the court himself and dunked the ball to lead the Bulls to a dramatic, historic 128–127 victory over the Celtics that forced an improbable Game 7.

That play confirmed Noah's place in Bulls history. He became the single-minded heart of the time and combined with '08 draft pick Derrick Rose to build a team that would reach the Eastern Conference Finals in '11. Noah was awarded a place on the NBA All-Defensive Second Team after the '10–11 season as the Bulls and coach Tom Thibodeau concentrated heavily on the defensive end of the game.

79 The Driver

If ever there was a case of "right place, right time," it belongs to George Koehler.

Koehler was a limousine driver from Chicago who happened to be at O'Hare Airport in Chicago one day in September 1984. He had a scheduled pickup that wasn't showing.

"I got a call to stick around for another flight...at 7:30," Koehler said. "As the pilot got off the 7:30 flight, I asked if more passengers were aboard. He said one more. I thought it was my customer. It was Michael [Jordan] instead."

Jordan was in Chicago to begin his life as a member of the Chicago Bulls following his draft-day pick by the Bulls back in June.

"I got excited," Koehler said. "I had followed his career. I told him I was waiting for a no-show, and I'd take him anywhere for $25. He said, 'Okay, you're on.'"

From that day forward, Koehler has been Jordan's designated driver, not just in Chicago, but around the world.

Koehler said Jordan looked uneasy that first day together.

"I don't know if he had been in a stretch limo before," Koehler told ESPNChicago.com. "He didn't know anybody in Chicago. I was a stranger and he was obviously a bit nervous that I might drop him off in an alley somewhere."

Koehler dropped Jordan at his destination, and Jordan paid him $50. Koehler offered his card and services anytime he was in Chicago, and two weeks later, Jordan called him, asking him to pick up his parents at O'Hare.

That relationship between driver and rider is still going on, although Koehler's role in Jordan's life has grown beyond the service aspect.

"If you picked up a book about Michael's life, it would be my life, just Michael's name on the cover," Koehler said.

Of all the hundreds of thousands of photos taken of Jordan, Koehler appears in the background of many. He was a constant companion to Jordan, occasionally serving as a bodyguard of sorts, sometimes a go-between for reporters and others who wanted a minute of Jordan's time.

"Of course, duties and responsibilities have shifted from limousine driving to all sorts of things for Michael," Koehler told the *Chicago Tribune* back in '99. "That's only because there are a lot of things that need to be done that Michael can't do himself. I don't mind doing that. [I have] a lot of great, fond memories of just hanging out and being Michael's friend."

Koehler's life was turned around, and probably significantly improved, because of a no-show at O'Hare.

80 *The Jordan Rules* (The Book)

When the Bulls won the NBA title for the first time in 1991, they were living in a wonderful world. Everyone loved Michael Jordan; Scottie Pippen was the kid from Arkansas who turned out to be a great defender; John Paxson was a local hero, the outside shooting threat; Bill Cartwright was the gruff but lovable giant; Horace Grant was just a big kid; and Phil Jackson was the genius coach who pushed all the right buttons. Chicago was Xanadu.

But it is never really like that, is it? There is always some tarnish on a golden bauble, and it was in the book *The Jordan Rules* that we found out about some of the backstage conflict.

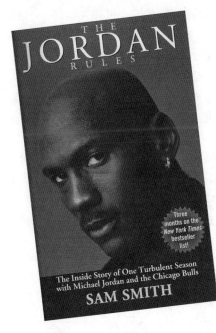

The Jordan Rules *went further toward explaining Jordan's otherworldly—some would say compulsive—need to win than anything that had come before.* (Triumph Books collection)

The Jordan Rules was written by Sam Smith, a longtime *Chicago Tribune* reporter who had covered the Bulls for a number of years for the newspaper. The '92 release of *The Jordan Rules* detailed the trials and tribulations of Jordan's ascension to the top of the NBA and the Bulls' struggles to meet his demands for coexisting talent.

The book told of Jordan's conflicts with both Bulls general manager Jerry Krause and coach Phil Jackson, of Jordan's dislike for the Triangle Offense forced onto the team by Krause, and of Jordan's constant battle to be the best he could be while demanding his teammates do the same.

There was also a damning exposé of the push to make Jordan the most famous athlete in the world through product endorsements. The back scenes of the advertising world were detailed.

The Jordan Rules told stories of Jordan's battle with teammates, including the time he threw a punch at one of them in practice.

Jordan's excessive need for competition came in story after story about scrimmage skirmishes.

The Jordan Rules also explained the details of the Jordan Rules, the defensive scheme hatched by the Detroit Pistons to beat the Bulls. The Pistons' Jordan Rules basically set out to make sure Jordan had to work overly hard for everything he got against Detroit, and had to face a barrage of physical attacks on his way to the basket if he so dare to go that way. The Jordan Rules were given credit for keeping the Bulls out of the NBA Finals until they finally broke through in '91.

The Jordan Rules book ended up having a wide effect on sports coverage in America, much as Jim Bouton's *Ball Four* did in baseball back in the '70s. Within the Bulls family, the book created rancor between general manager Jerry Krause, coach Phil Jackson, and assistant coach Johnny Bach, with questions as to who was responsible for giving author Smith his information.

It also caused Jordan to be cautious about his behavior and to create a tighter inner circle of friends and associates. The examinations from *The Jordan Rules* caused people to look at Jordan differently, and that examination took a leap when Jordan retired in '93 amid reports of a gambling addiction.

The book received mostly positive reviews. One of the more detailed reviews came from Fred Barnes in the *American Spectator*: "It's fair to compare *The Jordan Rules* with the campaign books that appear after every presidential race. A riveting account [of] what you want in a sports book: the behind-the-scenes stuff, a peek at the private side of the players, their hobbies and politics and religion, the way they get along and the way they don't."

Smith continued to cover the NBA for the *Tribune* for many years. After leaving the newspaper, he became the website reporter for bulls.com, the team's official website.

81 57 Wins!!!

In the early years of the NBA, before free agency was quite as "free" as it is today, teams usually grew slowly. But the Bulls made a big leap in just two years, going from a losing team in their first four seasons to a 50-win team in 1970–71.

With a starting lineup of Bob Love, Chet Walker, Tom Boerwinkle, Jerry Sloan, and Bob Weiss, the Bulls were primed to take the next step. The '71–72 season promised to be the best one in team history, and it was.

The Bulls were riding a high from the previous season, when they won 51 games. They added to their roster in the college draft that summer, selecting Kennedy McIntosh of Eastern Michigan in the first round. In the second round they picked up Willie Sojourner from coach Dick Motta's former workplace, Weber State, and Howard Porter from Villanova, who was coming off his impressive NCAA tournament performance. In the third round, they got center Clifford Ray from the University of Oklahoma, who turned out to be the real prize of the draft.

In November, the Bulls reacquired Norm Van Lier in a trade with Cincinnati for center Jim Fox, and he became the regular starting point guard in place of Weiss, who was moved to a sixth-man position.

The '71–72 season was one of the most interesting in NBA history, as the league was battling with the American Basketball Association over players and coaches. The ABA's Dallas franchise was wooing Motta to change leagues. Motta stayed, but forced then-Bulls scout Jerry Krause to leave the organization because the two never got along. In Motta's mind, he always believed he knew more about evaluating talent and Krause was just in the way.

Norm Van Lier raises up for a jumper against the Lakers in Game 1 of the 1972 Western Conference Finals. (Getty Images)

Krause would return years later to become general manager and designer of the greatest team in basketball history.

The Bulls lost the opener that season to Philadelphia but won the next five games. They had only one three-game losing streak the entire season, and that came in early November. They went 10–1 during one stretch early in the season to raise their record to 17–6 and went on from there to finish 32 games above .500, at 57–25. That was the most wins the club would have until the 1990–91 team won 61 games on the way to the franchise's first world championship.

Defense wins, and the '71–72 team proved it. It was the best defensive team in the league, holding opponents to 102.9 points per game (the Bulls averaged 111.2 on their end). Chet Walker scored a team-record 56 points in a win over Cincinnati. Ray made the NBA All-Rookie team, and Bob Love made the NBA Western Conference All-Star team, leading the team in scoring with 25.8 points per game.

Unfortunately for the Bulls, they were still in the same division and conference as the Milwaukee Bucks, who won 63 games that year, so the Bulls were matched again with the Los Angeles Lakers, who were led by an aging but still strong Wilt Chamberlain. The Lakers won 69 games in '71–72, a league record that stood until the '95–96 Bulls won 72 games.

Tom Boerwinkle, the team's incredibly dependable center, suffered a knee injury late in the regular season. Ray, who was good but only a rookie, had to play center in the first round playoff series, and the Lakers swept the playoff series.

Although the Bulls would not see 57 wins again for a long time, they did have greater playoff success in the '74–75 season, when they came one play away from making the NBA Finals.

The Shot (Utah)

In the 1997 NBA Finals, Steve Kerr hit a jumper from the top of the key to win Game 6 against the Utah Jazz and complete the Bulls' fifth title run. In '98, it was Michael Jordan's turn.

Jordan was known for hitting clutch shots in his career, but was actually better known for how he scored than when he scored. His high-flying dunks, his acrobatic moves to the hoop, his determination to break a defender's ankles, those were the key components of who Michael Jordan was. Last-second shots had occurred, but were not the most important aspect of the Jordan legacy.

By '98, Jordan was more earthbound, more of a team player, and definitely an elder statesman in the league. He had solidified his status as the greatest player ever by coming back from an initial retirement and reinventing himself physically, driving the Bulls to titles in '96 and '97 to go with the first three-peat.

In the '97 Finals—the first time the Bulls faced the Jazz—it was Jordan who passed the ball to Kerr for the 20-foot jumper that put the Bulls in the lead for good in the game's final seconds.

By '98, the reports were widespread that the Bulls were about to finish their dominant run in the NBA. The league was set for labor strife as a new collective bargaining agreement was required, coach Phil Jackson and general manager Jerry Krause were no longer friends, and Jordan and Dennis Rodman were playing on one-year contracts. Scottie Pippen had bristled at not getting the lucrative contract he wanted.

So it came down to June 14, 1998, with the Bulls leading the NBA Final series three games to two.

The Bulls trailed by three points when Jordan made a driving layup to pull the Bulls within a point. At the other end of the floor, as Utah's Karl Malone set up in his usual low-post spot, waiting for the moment he would turn and shoot his signature jumper, Jordan snuck around behind him, stole the ball, and quickly dribbled downcourt, hoping to create a scoring opportunity before the Jazz could set up their defense.

Dribbling the ball at the top of the key to the left side, Jordan looked up at Utah shooting guard Bryon Russell, who was guarding him. Jordan went to his right, toward the middle of the floor, bringing Russell along with him. Jordan put his hand on Russell, giving him a slight push out of the way, then hit the 18-foot jumper that gave the Bulls an 87–86 lead with 5.2 seconds remaining.

As Jordan's shot went through the hoop, he stood on the spot of the shot, with his right hand outstretched, as if he was not only completing the shot but also completing a career. He was allowing history to record a final moment, and hundreds of photographs were taken of Jordan admiring his shot, with the shooting hand extended. In the Jordan history of shots, the picture of him standing just beyond the free throw line with his hand outstretched is considered one of the all-time classics.

The most famous photograph of Jordan's shot (the shot of the shot, as it were) comes from behind Jordan, as he is looking at the ball heading toward the basket. NBA photographer Fernando Medina's shot was used in a book titled *Basketball's Best Shots.*

"What makes this shot fascinating is the multitude of facial expressions seen on the fans behind the basket," Medina wrote. "It's an interesting study of humanity. You have fans screaming, while others hold their heads or faces, fearing the worst. Some seem resigned to the outcome."

From the Utah point of view, Jordan committed an offensive foul that did not get called.

"Whether he pushed off or not, he was making that shot," Russell said of the moment.

Jordan's shot meant the Bulls won three of their six NBA championships with dramatic last-second shots: John Paxson's three-pointer to win Game 6 in Phoenix in '93, Kerr's basket in the '97 Finals, and Jordan's '98 winner.

The shot was the last one Jordan took as a Bull, and was expected to be the last one he would take as an NBA player. He retired again when the new CBA was signed early in '99, only to come back a year later with the Washington Wizards.

 **The Hand Switch**

There is sometimes a play in professional basketball that defies description and remains forever etched in the minds of those who saw it occur. Even in replay, these single acts of physical supremacy and athletic grace cause one to wonder about the true existence of gravity.

There are two great examples of this phenomenon in NBA history. The first was Julius Erving's most famous layup. Dr. J. jumped from behind and to the right of the backboard, seemingly floating, with the majority of his body (along with the ball) out of bounds, until he reached the left side, where he scooped the ball up off the backboard for a seemingly simple bank shot.

The second example is known as Michael Jordan's hand switch.

With just under eight minutes to go in the fourth quarter of Game 2 of the 1991 NBA Finals against the Lakers at Chicago Stadium, Jordan took off from the free throw line with the ball

The Tongue

Perhaps Michael Jordan would have been just as famous, just as heralded, if had kept his tongue in his mouth.

But he didn't.

When Jordan was serious about scoring, usually eyeing his competition dribbling the ball, preparing for the attack, he would stick his tongue all the way out of his mouth. It was a disconcerting look, and appeared to be dangerous, at least for the tongue, but it was Jordan's way, and he maintained that look throughout his career.

"My father used to have his tongue out when he'd be working, doing mechanical stuff," Jordan said. "I just picked it up from him. Coach [Dean] Smith wanted me to stop it when I was back at [North Carolina]. But it's not a conscious thing."

Of all the things that Jordan could do, like dunk the basketball, switch hands on the way up to the hoop, make improbable passes or steals, the tongue is one thing any youngster can impersonate on the playground.

Not that anyone would suggest they do so.

"I'm afraid they will bite them off," Jordan said in warning.

---

in his right hand. He jumped toward the basket as if to dunk the ball over the interior defense of the Lakers. When Sam Perkins of the Lakers (Jordan's former teammate at North Carolina) jumped to block the shot in that direction, Jordan transferred the ball to his left hand and laid the ball on the backboard for a layup on the other side. To some, the basket became known as "The Move."

"That will make every highlight for the next 10 years," said Bulls announcer Jim Durham, who undersold the shot by several decades.

"I first intended to dunk the ball," Jordan said. "Once I got up in the air I didn't think I had enough room. I thought I was going to fall short of the rim, so I switched hands and laid it in. I probably couldn't duplicate it if I tried."

The basket came during a 15–2 scoring streak for the Bulls that helped them claim the game and tie the series at one game apiece heading to Los Angeles, where they won three straight to claim their first NBA title.

It was just one basket in an incredible night for Jordan, who made 15 of 18 shot attempts, and added 13 assists and seven rebounds. That shot did not win the series, but it punctuated the fact that Jordan was on a mission to win a title, and nothing, including the law of gravity that affects normal humans, was going to stand in his way.

Amazingly, Los Angeles Lakers star guard Kobe Bryant impersonated Jordan's hand switch on a couple of occasions during his career, although Bryant's move failed to match Jordan's in one aspect. A search of the two shots on youtube.com will show that Bryant went for a right-handed layup before switching to the left hand, where Jordan appeared to be going for a dunk before he made the hand switch. Jordan's move appears much more difficult.

Artis Gilmore

From 1967 to 1976, the NBA had a rival for the attention of basketball fans in America. The American Basketball Association (ABA) set up shop in cities the NBA had not yet entered and presented basketball with a bit more flair than the NBA offered.

Some great NBA players got their starts in the ABA, including Julius Erving, George Gervin, Moses Malone, and Connie Hawkins. One of the better players in the ABA was Artis Gilmore, a 7'2" center out of Jacksonville University. Gilmore had led the Dolphins to the '70 NCAA title game, where they lost to UCLA, like everyone did back then.

While playing for the Kentucky Colonels of the ABA, he managed to accomplish a rare feat. He was named the league's Rookie of the Year and its MVP in '72. While in the league, he was named to the All-ABA First Team all five seasons, and was the MVP of the playoffs when the Kentucky Colonels defeated the Indiana Pacers for the '75 title.

While the Colonels drafted Gilmore for the ABA, the Bulls had drafted him for the NBA. He chose to go to the ABA because the contract offer was greater. But when the league folded in '76, four teams were absorbed into the NBA (the New Jersey Nets, San Antonio Spurs, Denver Nuggets, and Indiana Pacers) and the other players were placed in a special dispersal draft. Thanks to their 24-win season in '75–76, the Bulls had the No. 1 pick and finally acquired Gilmore.

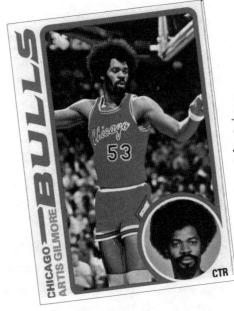

Gilmore manned the middle for six years in Chicago, averaging over 20 points per game during that period.
(Triumph Books collection)

Gilmore's arrival also seemed to mark the beginning of a new chapter for the Bulls. Bob Love had been traded to the New York Nets (the new NBA franchise), Jerry Sloan and Chet Walker were both long gone, and the Bulls were hoping first-round draft pick Scott May from the national champion Indiana Hoosiers would be the cornerstone of a new era.

Instead, it was Gilmore who kept the Bulls in play. At 7'2", 240 pounds, Gilmore was the dominating force in the middle the Bulls had been looking for since day one. While with the Bulls for six seasons, Gilmore averaged 19.3 points per game, with a high of 23.7 points in '78–79. He made the All-Star team four times as a Bull.

Gilmore led the Bulls on a strangely successful run to end the '76–77 season, when they won 20 of 24 games to make a short playoff run. They lost the three-game first round series in Game 3 against the eventual champion Portland Trail Blazers when a last-minute play went awry. An inbounds pass from guard John Mengelt was supposed to bounce off the backboard with Gilmore grabbing the rebound for a tying basket. Instead, the ball went in the hoop for a violation, and the Bulls lost the game.

The Bulls traded Gilmore to San Antonio (the former ABA franchise) in 1982 for center Dave Corzine and forward Mark Olberding. He came back to Chicago for part of his last professional season, but played just 24 games.

Gilmore, who played 17 professional seasons, suffered along with the Bulls, whose greatest success with Gilmore was in his first season, when the team came out of nowhere after a very slow start to make the playoffs. In his six full seasons with the Bulls, the team made the playoffs only twice.

Gilmore was inducted into the Basketball Hall of Fame in 2011.

85 Uniforms and Shoes

Although the material has changed dramatically, the Chicago Bulls are still wearing basically the same uniform they wore when the team was started back in the mid-1960s.

The Bulls still wear a white home uniform that reads "Bulls" on front with the number underneath. They wear a red road uniform with the same lettering on the front. They also have a black alternate uniform that is used when the team and league designate. Unlike the red and white uniforms, the pinstripe black jerseys say "Chicago" on the front rather than "Bulls." The black uniforms were a marketing ploy by the league started during the insanely exciting '95–96 season to sell more jerseys and take advantage of the Beatles-like popularity of the Bulls. The pinstripe was eliminated during the '99–00 season, replaced by a more flat black.

The Bulls also have a green uniform that was first used in '06 as a St. Patrick's Day special occasion, again with the idea of selling more jerseys. The Boston Celtics and New York Knicks, like Chicago representing cities with heavy Irish populations, also had green uniforms made up for the occasion. Since '06, the Bulls have worn the green jerseys a number of times.

On the legs of the shorts is a Bulls logo sitting inside a diamond cut.

In '09, the NBA started a campaign to attract more Hispanic fans and created a "Noche Latina" celebration. The Bulls were one of the teams to participate, and their red road uniforms for those occasions read "Los Bulls" on the front. Several other NBA teams also participated by coming up with new uniforms.

In '89, the Bulls also made a statement with their shoes.

The Bulls were beginning to feel the stirrings of a championship team. They had enjoyed their second consecutive winning season, and they were hoping to advance beyond the second round of the playoffs, which is where the Detroit Pistons ended their hopes the previous year.

So with another series against the Cleveland Cavaliers on the schedule for the start of the '89 playoffs, Bulls forward Brad Sellers had an idea: he suggested the Bulls all play in black shoes.

This was a revolutionary thought at the time. Most players wore shoes that were mostly white with only a little color, usually tied into the team's colors. Michael Jordan created a controversy earlier in his career when the first Air Jordans came out and they were almost entirely red with black trim and no white. He had been fined per game for wearing them for half a season.

But the Bulls showed up with black shoes on for the '89 playoffs, and they started a trend in the NBA.

The shoes were not immediately popular with the entire team, especially the Caucasian players, who stated publicly that the shoes made them look weighty and ponderous. They didn't really have that effect, but the look is one of the reasons nobody

The Astronaut Draft

It wasn't until the draft was over that people realized what the Bulls did in 1977.

With the 13th pick of the draft, the Bulls drafted Tate Armstrong from Duke. In the second round they picked Mike Glenn of Southern Illinois, the 23rd pick overall. Later in the second round, with the No. 30 pick overall, the Bulls selected Steve Sheppard from Maryland.

So what's so special about that? None of those players turned out to be very good players in the NBA.

But they did happen to have the same last name as three very famous astronauts: Neil Armstrong, John Glenn, and Alan Shepard. That's why the '77 Bulls draft became known as the Astronaut Draft.

had worn black shoes regularly in the NBA before the Bulls started doing it.

For the '96 playoffs, with Michael Jordan back and healthy and the Bulls coming off their record-breaking 72-win season, the Bulls went even further, wearing both black shoes and black socks. The look worked for Jordan, not so well for others.

86 Jersey Numbers

Okay Mr. (or Ms.) Know-It-All, do you know all the jersey numbers Michael Jordan wore as a Bull?

The jersey No. 23 is famous, of course, and is the one that will always be identified with Jordan, no matter who else wears that number for any other team in any other sport. That jersey number was retired by the Bulls in a ceremony on November 1, 1994, at the United Center, three nights before the first regular-season game played at the UC.

But when Jordan returned from his first retirement in the spring of '95, he wanted to honor his slain father, saying his father had witnessed his last game in the No. 23 jersey and he wanted to keep it that way. So he chose jersey No. 45, which was his junior high baseball number and the number he wore in his minor league baseball career.

In the first game of the Eastern Conference semifinals against Orlando, Jordan's physical condition, slowed by a year and a half away from the game, was exposed by Orlando's Nick Anderson, who stole the ball from Jordan late in the game that led to the winning basket. For the second game of the series, Jordan switched back to

No. 23 as a good luck charm, and he maintained that number the rest of his career, including his time with the Washington Wizards.

It was in Orlando that Jordan had an interesting jersey experience. He arrived at the Orlando Arena for a game against the Magic and discovered that his jerseys had been stolen. Luckily, Bulls equipment manager John Ligmanowski always carried a spare uniform for such emergencies.

So Jordan played in jersey No. 12 that night.

Jordan also wore jersey No. 9 while with the U.S. Olympic basketball Dream Team in '92.

Interestingly, the Chicago Cubs have also retired jersey No. 23, worn by second baseman Ryne Sandberg. During the first decade of the 2000s, the most famous Bears player was kick-returner Devin Hester, who set league records for touchdowns scored from kickoffs and punts and wore jersey No. 23.

Scottie Pippen's No. 33 jersey followed him to Houston, Portland, and Europe, where he played for a short while at the end of his career. Pippen's jersey was retired by the Bulls in December '05. While with the Dream Team, Pippen wore No. 8.

The first retired jersey for the Bulls was the No. 4 worn by Jerry Sloan when he was a player with the Bulls from 1966 to 1976. His jersey number was retired in '78, a year before Sloan became head coach of the team.

In '94, the Bulls retired the jersey number for Bob Love, who wore No. 10 when he played for the Bulls from 1968 to 1976. Oddly, Bulls guard B.J. Armstrong was wearing No. 10 at the time, and he was allowed to keep that jersey number until he left the Bulls in '95.

The jersey numbers are noted on banners that hang from the rafters at the United Center. Alongside those jersey number banners are banners celebrating the Bulls careers of coaches Johnny "Red" Kerr (who was also a team broadcaster for 32 years) and Phil Jackson (who coached the team for 11 years, two as an assistant and nine as head coach), as well as general manager Jerry Krause, who built the championship teams during his 18 years with the club.

87 Benny the Bull

Professional sports teams often feel the need for a mascot, and such was the case for the Bulls when they started off in the NBA in the late 1960s. With a name like "Bulls," a mascot seemed simple enough, assuming one could envision a two-legged Bull.

In '69, as ownership of the team changed hands, Philadelphia 76ers business manager Pat Williams was hired as general manager on the recommendation of renowned Chicago showman Bill Veeck. Williams, a protégé of Veeck, was known for his showmanship as well as his basketball acumen, and he immediately saw the need for a physical representation of the bull, so he started looking for an appropriate mascot.

Benny the Bull was named after Ben Bentley, a famed Chicago newspaperman who was the Bulls' first public relations man. A strange, seemingly makeshift costume (Chet Walker called it "a pitiful moth-eaten costume") was purchased, and Benny the Bull showed up on the sideline for games in '69. The first Benny looked nothing like the friendly faced, bouncy Benny the Bull that became popular in the '80s.

The Bulls believe Benny was the first NBA mascot roaming the sidelines of a league game. Because of the newness of this entertainment feature, the rules for mascots' behavior and movements were being etched out game by game sometimes. Benny was ejected from Game 4 of the Bulls-Milwaukee second-round playoff series in '74. His ejection came at the same time coach Dick Motta and injured star guard Jerry Sloan were tossed for yelling at the referees.

At some point, Benny was recreated into a lovable muffin of a mascot. He was big, standing about 6½ feet tall, and the team had two men who shared the job of being Benny. Benny did skits during timeouts, entertained fans in the stands, and was at every team function. Kids loved the smiley-faced mascot, and anyone who ever called themselves a Bulls fan had his or her picture taken with Benny somewhere along the line.

During the '80s, Benny became the most beloved mascot in Chicago (neither the Bears, Cubs, or White Sox had a real mascot at the time).

While Benny was entertaining fans in Chicago, a far more athletic mascot was becoming wildly popular in Phoenix. The Suns mascot, the Gorilla, would do dunks and put his body in harm's way to entertain the fans. Similar mascots popped up around the league, forcing the Bulls to make a change.

So in 2004, Benny got a cousin of sorts, an angrier, leaner mascot known as Da Bull. He came out to do acrobatic stunts and would often come into the arena from up above, hanging from guide wires to show team spirit.

Eventually, the Da Bull mascot became known as Benny the Bull. The softer, rounder mascot remained with the team in other forms, like when fans would crawl inside an inflatable Benny costume and race other similarly bedecked fans up and down the floor during timeouts.

Benny currently performs with a team of acrobatic dunk artists as well. The group is known as Benny and the Elevators and can be seen every so often at Bulls games.

88 Ron Harper

During the Bulls' first three-peat, Michael Jordan's running mate at the guard position was John Paxson, who showed his abilities during the 1991 finals against the Los Angeles Lakers and hit the game and NBA Finals series-winning shot against the Phoenix Suns in '93.

After Jordan retired, the Bulls had to rebuild their backcourt. B.J. Armstrong was already in place, filling in for the aging Paxson, and veteran shooting guard Pete Myers was hired to replace Jordan. In '94–95, veteran guard Ron Harper was signed to a long-term contract to be Jordan's replacement. When Jordan returned to active duty in March '95, he, Harper, and Armstrong ran the backcourt positions.

In June '95, Armstrong was selected by the Toronto Raptors in the expansion draft, and the team decided Harper and Jordan would be the team's new backcourt duo. Since neither was really a point guard, duties were a tad confusing, and some growth was needed.

As a collegian, Ron Harper was a thrill to watch. His relationship with gravity seemed tenuous, as he played above the rim while scoring 24 points per game during his senior year at Miami of Ohio.

In the '86 collegiate draft, the Cleveland Cavaliers decided to gain favor with local fans by drafting the native Ohioan with the eighth-overall pick. The Cavaliers were good, with the lineup of Brad Daugherty, Larry Nance, Mark Price, and John Williams, which is well-known to Bulls fans.

Harper scored 22.9 points per game in his rookie season to lead the Cavaliers, and finished second in the NBA Rookie of the Year balloting to Indiana's Chuck Person.

Harper was on the Cavaliers through the '88–89 season. In '88, his Cavaliers lost to the Bulls in a competitive five-game series in the first round of the playoffs, and in '89 he was again on the Cavs when Jordan hit the game-winning shot over Craig Ehlo to win yet another first-round series for the Bulls. Harper was endlessly compared to Jordan in those games and always came up wanting.

After three years with Cleveland, Harper was sent to the wasteland known as the Los Angeles Clippers, for whom he played five seasons. In '90, he suffered a severe knee injury that kept him out of the game for much of the next two seasons, and there was concern about his scoring ability upon his return. But from the '90–91 to the '93–94 season, he averaged over 18 points per game, topping out at 20.1 points per game in the '93–94 campaign.

In '94, the Bulls were still reeling from Michael Jordan's sudden retirement, and they signed Harper to a free agent contract to be their starting shooting guard. For some reason, Harper was a disappointment his first season, when he averaged just 6.9 points per game.

With the return of Jordan, the Bulls had to decide who was going to be the point guard and who was going to be the shooting guard, and Harper took over the point. Jordan and Harper shared guard responsibilities for the most part, and Harper became the starting guard for three NBA championship teams. After so many years as his team's main scorer, Harper decided to take a back seat in the offensive department and concentrated on his defensive abilities. He remained the team's starting guard for all three championship teams and contributed 9.3 points per game in the '97–98 season.

When the dynasty broke up in '98, Harper played one more season with the Bulls, then joined Phil Jackson with the Lakers, where he won two more NBA titles.

Harper was a gangly 6'6", and was very easy-going. Like former Bulls great Bob Love before him, Harper suffered from a lifelong problem with stuttering and was reluctant to do interviews unless he knew the reporter well.

89 Jordan's Kids

Michael and Juanita Jordan have three children: Jeffrey Michael Jordan, Marcus James Jordan, and Jasmine Jordan. They were raised in the Jordan home in Highland Park, Illinois, a pleasant, high-brow suburb north of Chicago.

The children all attended Loyola Academy, a private Roman Catholic High School in Wilmette, where the boys played basketball and Jasmine competed in gymnastics. Marcus transferred to Whitney Young High School for his junior and senior year after Jeffrey graduated from Loyola. Marcus led Whitney Young to the state title in 2009.

Being the children of the greatest basketball player in the history of the game, it might seem natural to take up the game as well. But there also had to be great pressure to perform, especially for the boys. Michael Jordan spoke of those pressures in his Hall of Fame speech.

"Jeffrey, Marcus, Jasmine, I love you guys," Jordan said. "You know I think that you guys have a heavy burden. I wouldn't want to be you guys if I had to, because of all the expectations that you have to deal with."

As the oldest, 6'1" Jeffrey faced the scrutiny first. Three of his senior-year basketball games were broadcast on ESPN. After graduating in the spring of '07, Jordan chose to be a preferred walk-on at the University of Illinois, passing up scholarship offers from Valparaiso and the University of Illinois-Chicago. For the '09–10 season, Jordan was offered a full scholarship to Illinois. But at the end of the '09–10 school year he decided to leave Illinois to attend the University of Central Florida, where Marcus was already enrolled.

Marcus, 6'3", attended UCF immediately after high school and created a stir in his first year when he refused to wear the school's assigned Adidas shoes, choosing instead to stick with his father's brand of Nikes. Adidas eventually ended its association with UCF as a result.

Jasmine reportedly was as skilled an athlete as her brothers but participated on the pom squad in high school as well as competed in gymnastics. She did not play basketball.

Michael and Juanita first filed for divorce in '02, reconciled for a short while, and then divorced for good in '06. Juanita reportedly received a settlement of $168 million in the divorce.

Luvabulls and Others

In 1979, the basketball world was ready for more entertainment. Sure, the games were fun, and Benny the Bull was a stitch. But the NBA was growing up, challenging the college game for the entertainment dollar, and they found a new way to one-up the talent seen at the collegiate level.

So the Bulls invented the Luvabulls, a dance team/cheerleading squad, to provide something to look at and watch during timeouts.

The Luvabulls quickly became one of the more entertaining aspects of the entire Bulls gameday experience.

The tryouts for the Luvabulls are reportedly intense, even though the women (they have to be 21 years of age or older) are paid a nominal per-game fee for being a member of the squad. They rehearse twice a week and have to show up well before the start of every Bulls game for another hour of rehearsals.

There are rewards, however. The Luvabulls have performed at tournaments across America and throughout Europe. They make hundreds of personal appearances a year, at conventions, trade shows, sales events, and charitable events as well.

Their dance numbers are at times entertaining and at other times almost risqué. They are beyond cheerleaders; they are professional dancers, but they are also skilled at precision dance moves. They compete against other NBA dance squads every summer.

The Bulls also have a Junior Luvabulls program for young girls who want to improve their dance skills and get a foot in the door for future Luvabulls tryouts.

Bulls games are busy events. There is entertainment during every timeout. Some of them are games shown on the huge video board above center court at the United Center, but others are live performances by regular contributors.

The IncrediBulls (who knew the team name would be so flexible for future use?) are a group of young men and women who entertain the crowds during timeouts. They usually enter the stands to get the crowd pumped up for the game by encouraging cheering, or playing games. They bring balloons, and often one of the IncrediBulls is wearing a basketball backboard above his head, allowing small children the chance to throw hand-sized basketballs at the board for an easy two-pointer. It's the IncrediBulls who provide the T-shirts shot out of one of those T-shirt cannons that are so popular at sporting events. Like the Luvabulls, the IncrediBulls often make appearances at events outside of the United Center.

The Stampede is a drum corps comprised of members from area drum and bugle corps. They perform occasionally at Bulls games and participate with the others in entertaining fans in the concourses before and during games.

The Bucket Boys, a Chicago institution, are a group of teenagers from the city's South Side who play complicated percussive sets on paint buckets. They performed for audiences in public for years before the Bulls discovered them and brought them inside for game celebrations. They are an inner-city urban phenomenon that has to be seen to be believed.

Then there are the Matadors, who also have to be seen to be believed. They are a group of heavyset Bulls fans who perform at games in much the same way as the Luvabulls do, with dance sets. They also perform in sometimes skimpy costumes, or perhaps costumes that are only skimpy because they are on the Matadors. Either way, they provide yet another form of entertainment.

Finally, there are the Swingin' Seniors, a group of elder Bulls fans who dance at center court when invited to do so.

All of these entertainers and more can be seen on the concourses outside the arena area before and after games. There are also two bands that perform before each game as well as magicians and puppeteers.

91 The Bus Ride to Milwaukee

By the end of the 1995–96 NBA season, the Bulls were more of a traveling circus than they had been during the first three-peat. The addition of Dennis Rodman, the excitement surrounding Michael Jordan's return to the NBA, and the devastating way the Bulls were plowing through the league made them the league equivalent of the Beatles.

They traveled first class all the way, with their own private plane, staying at the fanciest possible hotels with the highest level of security. It was impossible for the average fan to get near them on most of their road trips.

When they went on the road, their games were the hottest ticket in town. For the Western Conference clubs who only got to see the Bulls once a year, the annual visit was the most significant sports event of the year.

Security for private airplanes is relatively easy, since the jets usually take off from remote locations at airports. But it makes no sense to fly from Chicago to Milwaukee, which is a 90-minute-max trip up I-94 West by car or bus.

So on April 16, 1996, the Bulls prepared to go to Milwaukee's Bradley Center for a game against the Bucks. Their most significant baggage was their 69–9 record through the first 78 games of the season.

If the Bulls beat the Bucks, as expected, they would become the first team in NBA history to win 70 games in a single season.

So the Bulls loaded up into their luxury bus on that Tuesday afternoon and took off from their Deerfield, Illinois, practice facility, the Berto Center, to get on the nearby interstate and get themselves to the lakeside community of Milwaukee, considered by some to be the northernmost suburb of Chicago.

The drive from Deerfield at first goes by some affluent north shore communities before getting to the Wisconsin border. After that, the route goes past Kenosha and Racine on the way to the beer capital of America.

On the way, there are several overpasses, with state roads crossing over the interstate. On this particular Tuesday, each of the overpasses was crowded with fans who stood above the interstate with banners draped over the barriers, prompting the Bulls to get the 70th win that night. The sight of the fan support was a surprise, and a huge lift for the Bulls on their way to Milwaukee.

"The first thing we noticed was that there were three helicopters following us," said Bulls center Bill Wennington in his '04 book *Tales from the Bulls Hardwood*. "They were from news stations and they were covering our trip up to Milwaukee. Then we noticed that whenever we would go under an overpass, there were people standing on the road above us. They were waiting to get a glimpse of our bus as it took us on the way to history."

The bus ride back to Chicago had a caravan of Bulls fans following as the city celebrated the history-making win.

92 Al Vermeil and Erik Helland

In the early days of the NBA, teams usually had one staff member who was responsible for everything from uniforms to equipment to the care and treatment of player ailments. In fact, Johnny "Red" Kerr, the Bulls' first coach, was the first to have a full-time assistant coach. He demanded that Baltimore Bullets teammate Al Bianchi be hired as an assistant coach as part of his agreement to go into retirement and coach the Bulls.

Trainers eventually became a staple for NBA teams, but those men were also required to make sure all of the uniforms and equipment were ready, and they usually also served as a traveling secretary for the team, arranging hotel rooms, buses, and cabs when necessary. It was a thankless 24/7 job.

Over the years, as the NBA became more profitable, teams built huge support staffs. There were separate individuals for uniforms and equipment, for weight training, for overall health care, and for treatment of injuries.

The first official trainer for the Bulls was Bob Biel, who joined the team in 1973. In '76 it was Doug Atkinson, who stayed with the team through '80. Then the Bulls hired Mark Pfeil, an energetic young trainer who was the first one to work on Michael Jordan when he joined the team in '84.

Bulls general manager Jerry Krause took unusual pride in the team's training staff and in '89 he added strength and conditioning coach Al Vermeil to the roster. Vermeil is the brother of former NFL coach Dick Vermeil, and he is the only known strength coach to have a world championship ring from both the National Football League and the National Basketball Association.

Vermeil had a similar work ethic to his brother. He was responsible for helping to increase the strength of not only Jordan but of his two pet projects, Horace Grant and Scottie Pippen, who entered the NBA as skinny forwards and left it as physical specimens.

Vermeil eventually was named to the initial Hall of Fame class in the Strength Coaches Hall of Fame in '03.

In '90, the Bulls hired a new trainer out of California named Chip Schaefer, who worked with the team through the championship years and then left the team along with Phil Jackson and continued his NBA career with the Jackson-led Lakers.

Vermeil eventually added to his staff by hiring young trainer Erik Helland, who had a special affinity for working with Bulls' big men such as Bill Cartwright, Will Perdue, Bill Wennington, and Luc Longley.

When the Bulls were first winning their titles in the early '90s, one of the traits they had going for them was good health. They were rarely injured. Michael Jordan played 82 games in '91, 80 games in '92, and 78 games in '93. Scottie Pippen missed just one game in those first three title years. Horace Grant missed 10 games in three seasons.

Jerry Krause, who once got in trouble for saying that "organizations win championships," tried to suggest that the Bulls were staying healthy because they had the best training staff in the league. Luck, apparently, had nothing to do with it.

Through the '80s, '90s, and into the 21st century, the Bulls have had the same equipment manager. John Ligmanowski owned the truly full-time job. He arrived hours before the players for home games, arranging uniforms that were usually laundered the night before, making sure the shoes were arranged properly, and all the other sundry equipment needs were met. Always in his signature shorts, Ligmanowski patrolled first the Chicago Stadium and then the United Center for many hours more than the coaches, players, or fans.

When Michael Jordan's jersey was stolen from his locker in Orlando one year, it was Ligmanowski who provided Jordan with the extra jersey (No. 12) he kept on hand for just such occasions.

Eventually, the Bulls got around to announcing the names of the training staff and equipment manager in the pregame introductions.

Superfans

Chicago is a unique city. From its birth as a trading post for Native Americans or ships coming into the ports from Lake Michigan, through its years as a central American stockyard and a center for manufacturing, Chicago became known for its ethnic diversity, its architecture, its museums, its music, and its food.

Eventually, Chicago became home to a comedy group called Second City, a comedic training ground that produced the starting point for numerous famous American comedic actors, including Bill Murray, John Belushi, and Tina Fey, among many others. Several other comedy troupes began in Chicago as well, and many actors and *Saturday Night Live* cast members got their start in Chicago.

In the summer of 1988, a Chicagoan named Robert Smigel, who eventually became a writer for *SNL*, invented a comedic act he called "Superfans," which performed in Chicago. The act consisted of a group of men wearing Chicago sports team jerseys, who would sit around a table drinking beer, smoking cigars, and discussing the fate of their favorite teams, all of them from Chicago.

Superfans got its first national exposure on *Saturday Night Live* in '91. The group that night was led by famous actor Joe Mantegna, also a native Chicagoan, and included Smigel.

The theme of the Superfans act was that they would sit around the table, wearing Bears jerseys, with bushy mustaches, and discuss Chicago sports the way other people might discuss politics or religion. They were purportedly gathered at a true-to-life Chicago sports bar/restaurant owned by former Chicago Bears coach Mike Ditka, the first idol for the Superfans.

The Superfans were all portly, out-of-shape men who loved to eat Polish sausage and drink beer. They all had heart conditions brought on by overeating. They all spoke with Chicago accents, referring to the Bears as "Da Bears" and Ditka as "Da Coach." In Superfans parlance, Ditka could do no wrong and could not be defeated in any endeavor. When discussing the Super Bowl Bears of '85, the Superfans would discuss who would win a contest of any

Chris Farley, Robert Smigel, Mike Myers, and George Wendt in an episode of "Bill Swerski's Superfans" on Saturday Night Live, *May 18, 1991.*

sort between the Bears and any opponent, with the Bears winning by exaggerated margins. Ditka in particular was often pitted against natural disasters or supernatural opponents with the Superfans predicting a Ditka win.

With the ascent of Michael Jordan and the Bulls, the Superfans also began to discuss the miracle of Michael Jordan in similar fashion. Both Ditka and Jordan appeared in Superfans skits on *Saturday Night Live*, and Jordan ended up in a hula skirt, doing the Hawaiian dance with the other Superfans.

When Jordan had his first retirement ceremony at the United Center in '94, two members of the Superfans showed up to discuss Jordan's legacy. The Superfans were also part of the Grant Park celebrations for each of the Bulls' first three titles in '91, '92, and '93.

And, in a case of life imitating art, while many would argue that Chicago fans didn't sound like the characters portrayed in the sketch, "Da Bulls," "Da Bears," and "Da Coach" became a part of the Chicago fan's vocabulary.

94 Favorite Starting Five

Now that you know the history of the Bulls (assuming you started from the front of the book), it's time for you consider your all-time Bulls starting five.

Are you ready?

Let's start at shooting guard. I think Michael Jordan would be a good one to put there. See, that was easy.

But coming up with a running mate for Jordan is not going to be as easy. Although Jordan often controlled the ball himself, there were teams for two decades before Jordan came along, and there have been teams since Jordan left.

So you and your friends can start the debate. Here are some of your candidates:

Norm Van Lier was the first point guard to stick with the Bulls for a number of years. Playing with Hall of Fame shooting guard Jerry Sloan (who just got ignored for the first All-Bulls team, by the way), Van Lier was popular for his hard-nosed playing style and his hip behavior off the court. Van Lier stayed around the team until his death, and his quick wit and sharp tongue made him a popular commentator.

Best Team Ever

The 1995–96 Bulls won a league-record 72 games, a record that many people believe will never be broken. As a result, many observers believe the Bulls from that season are the best single-season team in NBA history.

But fans of former teams from Boston and Los Angeles will argue that point. They say that the '71–72 Lakers, who won 33 consecutive games with Jerry West, Gail Goodrich, and Wilt Chamberlain, were a better team. That team held the victories record of 69 until the Bulls won their 72 games 24 years later.

Then there was the '85–86 Boston Celtics, which included Larry Bird and four other future Hall of Famers, including Robert Parish and Kevin McHale. Or how about the '86–87 Lakers, which included a lineup with Magic Johnson, Kareem Abdul-Jabbar, and James Worthy?

Well, the question got answered in the spring of 2011, when the legendary American sports magazine *Sporting News* selected the greatest teams from the four major sports and chose the '95–96 Bulls as the No. 1 team in NBA history.

The magazine cited the team's 105.2 points per game average and the fact that it was the best in the league in scoring efficiency and defensive efficiency.

The '71–72 Lakers got the No. 2 spot. The '86–87 Lakers got the No. 3 spot, and the aforementioned Celtics were selected No. 4.

The magazine asked an all-star panel of current and former coaches, players, executives, and writers to help select the winner.

The Bulls from '91–92, which beat Portland in the NBA Finals after winning 67 games, was selected as the No. 9 team of all time.

From the championship years, your choices are John Paxson and Ron Harper. Paxson was more of a true point guard, while Harper sort of fit a role designated by Jordan's move to point guard.

Then there is Derrick Rose, who popped onto the scene in 2008, became the league's Rookie of the Year in his first year, and the youngest MVP ever in his third.

You are going to have a nice conversation when you get to small forward, between Hall of Famer Scottie Pippen and Bob Love, the Bulls' first superstar. Both players have had their jersey numbers retired by the Bulls. You also have to give some consideration to Toni Kukoc, who was the NBA's Sixth Man of the Year and could have started for any team other than the championship Bulls. Also, Luol Deng was a member of the Bulls for most of a decade after the dynasty ended.

At power forward, your candidates are probably three-time champion Horace Grant, three-time champion Dennis Rodman, and Chet Walker, who was an NBA champion before he was a Bull in the early '70s. Rodman, a seven-time rebounding champion, was elected into the Hall of Fame in 2011, which might sway votes his way (though Walker also went into the Hall in 2012).

Then we get to the most troubling position in Bulls history, the center position. For the championship teams, the starters were Bill Cartwright the first three years and Luc Longley the second three.

But Tom Boerwinkle patrolled the middle for the Bulls an entire decade, and Artis Gilmore was a superstar before and during his time with the Bulls. Go ahead, make your pick.

Once you select your starting five, the other candidates can be thrown into the mix for your bench players. Keep Sloan in mind, since he is a Hall of Famer and has had his jersey retired. Don't forget the likes of Ben Gordon and Kirk Hinrich from the post-dynasty era, or early contributors like David Greenwood and Reggie Theus. Or do you want to fill your entire roster with Bulls champions like Stacey King and Ron Harper?

The great thing is, you have a lot of players to choose from.

95 Players Denied Titles

From 1991 through 1998, the NBA held eight playoffs and the Bulls won six. The Bulls won three titles in a row from '91 through '93, took two years off while Michael Jordan played baseball, then won three more between '96 and '98.

In between, the Houston Rockets, led by star center Hakeem Olajuwon, won back-to-back titles. In '94 they defeated Patrick Ewing's Knicks and in '95 they defeated the Orlando Magic.

So for eight years the NBA title was won by two franchises. That means for eight years many talented players for 28 other teams were denied titles.

There are always great players in any league who never win titles. Whether it is a matter of timing, the lack of quality teammates, bad management, or bad fortune, many, many professional athletes finish their professional careers without a ring.

But because of the domination of the Bulls, and the good timing of the Rockets, several great NBA players went their entire careers without an NBA title. The Bulls directly affected the opportunity for good players to become champions.

Ewing was a great example. Ewing played 17 seasons in the NBA. He was twice an Olympic gold medalist. He was selected to the NBA's top 50 players of all time. He became a Hall of Famer in '08, alongside Olajuwon.

But he never won an NBA title. The Bulls eliminated his team in '89 in the conference semifinals and did it again in '91 in the first round of the playoffs. They met again in the '92 Eastern Conference semifinals, then again in the conference finals in '93.

In '94, with Jordan retired, the Knicks got lucky in beating the Bulls in the conference semifinals, but Ewing's Knicks could not get past Olajuwon's Rockets. With Jordan back, the Bulls eliminated Ewing's team in the conference semifinals in '96.

Another player who could not win because of Jordan was one of Jordan's best friends, Charles Barkley. Like Ewing, he was a gold medal Olympian and one of the 50 best players ever. But whether he was in Philadelphia or in Phoenix, Barkley could not get past the Bulls.

In both '90 and '91, Barkley's 76ers lost to the Bulls in the Eastern Conference semifinals, both times by 4–1 margins. They didn't stand a chance. Then Barkley got traded to the Phoenix Suns for the '92–93 season, and he got the team all the way to the NBA Finals, only to meet up with the Bulls again.

It was John Paxson's three-pointer in Game 6 in Phoenix that sealed the deal in that series, when Barkley's Suns had home-court advantage and would have hosted Game 7.

Two more Hall of Famers were denied by the Bulls. Karl Malone and John Stockton formed one of the great duos in NBA history for the Utah Jazz, and both went to the Hall of Fame. Yet again, they were like Ewing and Barkley, with Olympic Gold Medals and places on the NBA's Best 50 players list.

But Jordan and the Bulls beat the Jazz in both the '97 and '98 NBA Finals. Malone's final season was '03–04, when he joined the Lakers hoping for a ring, but they were beaten by the Detroit Pistons in the Finals that year.

One other player who suffered at the hands of the Bulls was shooting guard Reggie Miller, the outspoken and stylish guard for the Indiana Pacers. The Bulls and Pacers only met in the playoffs once during the championship years, but it was a historic series that went to seven games. It was in the '98 Eastern Conference Finals, and the Bulls won Game 7 at home by five points to advance and end Miller's dream.

The Bulls stood in the way of center Shaquille O'Neal early in his career until Jordan retired, the dynasty broke up, and O'Neal got his chance to be a champion.

96 Record Holders

Did you like taking history classes in school? For some people, the study of history is an exciting reminder of where we have been. For others it is a bore, trying to make old times matter.

But when it comes to sports, history matters a great deal. It is the history of a team, or a sport, that comes up in conversation time and again, as fans try to compare one era to another, or remember the great players and teams from a different time.

The Chicago Bulls have a history before Michael Jordan joined the team, and before the Bulls won six titles in the 1990s. Want proof? Go to the Internet and look up the Bulls record book.

Certainly, there are Bulls team records that Jordan holds and may never be broken. He is the team leader in points scored, games played, minutes played, field goals made, field goals attempted, free throws made, free throws attempted, total rebounds, total assists, and total steals.

He also leads the team in turnovers, but let's not dwell on that.

Scottie Pippen, by the way, is second in almost all of those categories. He also leads the team in career personal fouls, but let's not dwell on that, either.

But it is Artis Gilmore who leads the team in field goal percentage (an astounding 58.7 percent) and guard Kirk Hinrich who leads the team in three-point field goals attempted and made. Steve

Kerr leads the team in three-point field goal percentage at another astounding figure of 47.9 percent.

Although Jordan is the career rebounding leader, Horace Grant is the team leader in offensive rebounds. Scottie Pippen is second in that category and Michael Jordan is third.

Tom Boerwinkle, by the way, is second in total rebounds, ahead of Pippen. Boerwinkle once had a team-record 33 rebounds in one game, so that kicks his total up some.

Jordan and Pippen are second and third behind Gilmore in career blocked shots.

Among the single-season team records, it might come as a surprise to find out that Michael Jordan ranks only third in minutes played in a single season. He is topped by Bob Love in '70–71 and Jalen Rose in '02–03.

Dennis Rodman holds all of the team's single-season rebounding records. The single-season record for assists goes to Guy Rodgers, who was the Bulls' first star player back in '66–67 when he had 908 assists. That is obviously the oldest record still on the books.

Artis Gilmore holds the team record for most turnovers in a season at 366 and, in a surprise perhaps, the team leader in single-season personal fouls is a tie between Boerwinkle in '68–69 and Mickey Johnson in '77–78. They each had 317 fouls in a single season. Dennis Rodman never even cracked the top 10 in that category.

Michael Jordan owns all of the top 10 seasons in points scored and field goals made. Bob Love breaks into the field goals attempted list one year to break Jordan's hold on that category.

The Next Jordan

Michael Jordan spoke at his Hall of Fame induction speech about how hard it would be for his boys Jeffrey and Marcus to succeed at basketball with the specter of their father's greatness hanging over them.

Jeffrey and Marcus could probably have gotten some words of advice from any number of players who came along after Jordan with the moniker of "The Next Jordan" hanging over their heads.

For many, it did not really take that long for the next Jordan to come along. Many fans, especially the younger ones, will tell you that Kobe Bryant is all Jordan ever was and more. It's a debate that will rage on forever, perhaps, and one that can never be settled.

But there were "The Next Jordans" before the first Jordan was even done playing.

Harold Miner, who played his college ball at the University of Southern California, was known for his dunking ability. He stood just 6'5", but his spectacular dunking ability helped him earn the nickname "Baby Jordan." He entered the NBA in '92, selected 12th overall by the Miami Heat.

Miner's NBA career was unspectacular, although he did twice win the Slam Dunk contest at the NBA's All-Star Game.

On numerous occasions, Miner spoke of the pressure that came with the "Baby Jordan" tag.

"I always felt the worst thing to happen to Harold was the 'Baby Jordan' tag," former USC coach George Raveling said.

One year after Miner entered the NBA, Penny Hardaway came into the league. He ended up in Orlando and played with Shaquille O'Neal, but even though he was considered an equal to

Jordan athletically, he could not produce points the way Jordan did. He also never grew physically, in terms of strength, the way Jordan did.

Once again, one year later, a very mature and talented player came out of Duke University. Grant Hill was compared to Jordan for numerous reasons: his size, his court awareness, his maturity. Hill spent six years in Detroit, suffered numerous injuries over the years, but resembled—if not duplicated—Jordan in many ways. He just wasn't as spectacular.

Jerry Stackhouse followed Jordan out of North Carolina and averaged 18 points per game in his 16-year career, but he couldn't shoot. He could score, but his shooting percentage ranged well below 40 percent for most of his career. Jordan, too, came out of college as a scorer and not a shooter, but he taught himself how to become a better shooter.

Another Tar Heel to suffer in constant comparison to Jordan was Vince Carter, a terrific scorer who could not, or would not, play satisfactory defense. He suffered as well from playing in Toronto for the first part of his career. Carter's scoring average of 21.4 percent for his career was higher than most "Next Jordans" to come out.

After a stellar defensive performance against the Chicago Bulls in the Eastern Conference Finals in 2011, LeBron James began to get comparisons to Jordan. Not that he was the same kind of player, but that he was better at some things than Jordan was. However, James disappeared in the NBA Finals against the eventual champion Dallas Mavericks, which should have been an obvious Jordan-esque moment, and such talk quickly ceased. Though his victory in the 2012 Finals against Oklahoma City will certainly rekindle some of the talk.

Early Ownership

The first owner of the Chicago Bulls was Dick Klein, who put together a group of financial investors to buy his way into the NBA. His efforts were often hindered by the league, which was wary of investors in Chicago after being burned once before by the Chicago Zephyrs. But when the ABC television network wanted to talk about a broadcast deal, it said it wanted a team in the populous Chicago area.

Before the 1972–73 season, the tenuous Bulls ownership situation was changed, and probably cemented. Klein lost many of his original financial supporters because the Bulls were not making money.

The team was eventually sold to an ownership group that included Chicago Blackhawks owner Arthur Wirtz, who had agreed to give the Bulls a home stadium when they were chased out of the Amphitheatre years earlier. Also in the group was New York Yankees owner George Steinbrenner, as well as Jonathan Kovler and NFL stalwart Lamar Hunt, who were in the original ownership group.

Klein made millions off the sale of his stock to the new group, but it pained him to leave his role in what he saw as the potential gold mine of professional basketball in Chicago.

"My mistake was having partners who weren't in it for the long pull," Klein said.

Wirtz got involved because it gave him two tenants for his Chicago Stadium through the winter. That way the building was working for him instead of against him half the time.

Unfortunately, the new ownership group included a number of men who were quite accustomed to making decisions. Therefore,

Pro Basketball in Chicago

The first known professional basketball team in Chicago was the Chicago Bruins, a team founded in 1925 by Chicago Bears founder and coach George Halas. The Bruins played in the American Basketball League, which lasted six years. The Bruins were the farthest west franchise in the league.

In '27, a man named Abe Saperstein created the Harlem Globetrotters, known around the world as one of the greatest continuous acts—and certainly the most successful sports-related entertainment group—of all time. Saperstein built the team in Chicago and they played their first game in a town far west of Chicago called Hinckley, but Saperstein named them Harlem after the New York neighborhood to give them a showy identity.

In '39, Halas reinstated the Bruins into the National Basketball League, but they lasted only another three years. Another Chicago team that played in the NBL was the Chicago American Gears, which started in '44, and in '46 signed DePaul University star George Mikan, who was 6'10" and wore glasses. The Gears won the '47 NBL title.

The Chicago Stags were one of the original teams in the Basketball Association of America, which was the predecessor to the NBA. The Stags lasted four years after being unable to make a dent in the Chicago sports entertainment market.

The NBA gave Chicago a franchise in '61, and owner Dave Trager named the team the Chicago Packers, representing Chicago's meat-packing industry. Future Hall of Famer Walt Bellamy played for the Packers, and was second in the league in scoring behind Wilt Chamberlain's unbelievable 50 points per game. The Packers went 18–62, and for the next season were renamed the Chicago Zephyrs. They finished 25–55 in '62–63, and then Trager moved his team to Baltimore to become the Bullets.

In the 2000s, prior to the economy-choking recession that occurred late in the first decade of the century, there was talk that Chicago could be host to a second NBA team, in much the same way the New York/New Jersey area and the Los Angeles area is. But that talk died down when the NBA began to suffer financially along with much of the rest of the country.

any decision that was to be made in regards to the Bulls, including player moves, had to go through the Gang of Seven, and each owner had to sign off on the deal. All of the trades from the mid-'70s to the mid-'80s were slowed and in some cases negated by the fact that general manager Pat Williams could not get quick approval to make the deals.

The same thing happened with the marketing of the team. Again, the entire ownership group had to sign off on any marketing plans, and Williams, a showman of the first order, grew weary of trying to get anything done. Wirtz was a hardcore hard-sell man who made his money during the Depression when the rest of the country was going under, and marketing meant little to him. The other owners followed his lead.

In '84, that group of owners sold the team to a group led by Jerry Reinsdorf, a real estate man from New York who had already purchased the Chicago White Sox.

 **Funniest Bull**

Michael Jordan is the greatest player ever to wear a Chicago Bulls jersey, and he may always be that. But there is one competition he would not ever be entered into: funniest Bull.

While Michael Jordan has a great sense of humor, and an infectious laugh that takes over his entire body, he was never known for cracking jokes or telling funny stories. He could play "the dozens" as well as anybody, taking pot shots at others in a friendly game of insult, but he wasn't an outwardly funny guy.

Now Stacey King, that's another story.

King entered the NBA in 1989 as a smallish left-handed center out of Oklahoma. He never managed to rise above that status much, although he was a key bench player on the first three championship teams. His size, and his inability to do anything with his right hand, held him up on the floor.

But nobody was funnier on the six championship teams than King, which is why he was able to turn his sense of humor into a new career as a broadcaster once his playing and coaching days were over.

King was a very good mimic, and with a quick open smile and a seemingly inoffensive manner, he could make anybody laugh. He had two regular targets for his humor, although he was more likely to crack wise when the opportunity presented itself than try to set himself up for jokes.

Bulls general manager Jerry Krause was an unfortunate target of jokes due to his standing with the team and his secretive nature, and King could impersonate Krause's grumbly voice patterns well. Similarly, King absolutely nailed his impersonation of Bulls center Bill Cartwright, who himself had a hardtack voice from basketball-related injuries over the years. What made King's impersonation of Cartwright so funny is that Cartwright, a very quiet and reserved man, would seethe when he heard it but never say anything about it.

The first funniest Bull was the first Bulls coach, Johnny "Red" Kerr. With his Irish sense of humor, Kerr found jokes everywhere, and cracked wise whenever he had the chance. He, too, turned his sense of humor into a broadcasting career that lasted over 30 years.

Winning made everybody laugh during the dynasty years, and there was always a lot of joking going on. Center Bill Wennington, an affable sort who rarely got angry, was always a media favorite because he was quick to offer a postgame quip.

In the post-dynasty era, the funniest Bull is easily Joakim Noah. While Noah isn't a jokester, his refusal to treat sports as life or death makes him a favorite of media as well.

Now back to Jordan.

In '88, the league introduced Miami into the NBA, and when the Bulls arrived in Miami for the first time, they were also introduced to another Florida phenomenon: Hooters Restaurant. The restaurant features tasty chicken wings served by buxom young women in revealing outfits, and Jordan and the Bulls were quick to sample the restaurant that first year.

Cliff Levingston and Stacey King crack each other up in practice, just prior to the Bulls matchup with the Trail Blazers in the 1992 NBA Finals.

235

The night of the first ever game in Miami, inside the Bulls locker room, the players were given their free ticket envelopes. They would put the name of their invited guest on the envelope, a Miami team employee would put tickets in the envelopes, and then the tickets would go to will call to await pick-up.

That night, Jordan made an announcement:

"Okay, guys. No tickets for Hooters Girls." Then he paused and said, "And I need 16 tickets right now."

100 Pat Williams

One of the great names in Chicago sports history is that of Bill Veeck. Veeck, a native Chicagoan and showman of the first order, owned the Chicago White Sox twice, and did his best to put a competitive team on the field while making money for himself and his investment group. He created a number of memorable baseball moments, like signing the first African-American player in the American League, Larry Doby, and signing former Negro League star pitcher Satchel Paige to a contract at an (undisclosed) advanced age.

Veeck, the former owner of the White Sox, knew of a young man working for the Philadelphia 76ers named Pat Williams. Williams was a good basketball mind, but like Veeck was as much a showman as sportsman. When the Bulls ownership group ousted first owner Dick Klein from the team picture, they needed a general manager and asked Veeck for a name. Veeck suggested Williams, who was hired immediately.

Williams immediately greased the skids for a key trade with the 76ers, in which veteran all-star Chet Walker was sent to the

Bulls. Walker spent his remaining years with the Bulls and with Bob Love, Jerry Sloan, and Norm Van Lier had the first long-term success for the franchise.

Williams created the team's mascot, Benny the Bull, and spent half his time improving the team and improving the gameday experience. He said although Blackhawks fans had no trouble going to the Chicago Stadium on the city's impoverished west side, basketball fans didn't want to go because there wasn't a sufficient crowd to guarantee safety. Williams said his job was to get enough people in the building that more would feel safe about coming.

But a combination of Williams' efforts and the team's greatest success on the court (they finished 51–31 in 1972–73), started producing crowds in five digits, and on March 16, 1973, they hosted a sellout of 18,519. It was their second sellout of the season, both against Milwaukee, and there was a sense that the Bulls were becoming a significant sports entity in town.

Unfortunately, Williams clashed often with Motta, who thought he knew more about basketball than anyone else. Motta first chased player scout Jerry Krause out of a job. (Krause would eventually return to become the team's general manager and architect of the six championship seasons.) When the Bulls ended up playing the Los Angeles Lakers in the first round of the '72–73 playoffs, Motta somehow blamed Williams for making his team fly out to the coast immediately after the end of the regular season. Williams left the team at the end of the season and became general manager of the Atlanta Hawks. He returned to Philadelphia and served as the general manager there, and his team won the '83 NBA championship. In '87, he served as co-founder of the Orlando Magic and remained a senior vice president of the club while building his own motivational speaking business.

Williams was named one of the NBA's 50 most influential people by *Beckett's* magazine in '96. He and his wife have 14 adopted children and five of their own, and he has written dozens of books, some on motivation and others on sports, including a book titled *How to Be Like Mike: Life Lessons About Basketball's Best.*

Sources

I'm a newspaper man. As such, I trusted in the newspapers of America for much of the information in this book. That I accessed the newspapers via the Internet doesn't change the fact that the information came from the ink-stained wretches who cover the National Basketball Association.

In particular, I took advantage of the archives of the *Chicago Tribune*, *Chicago Sun-Times*, and the *Daily Herald*, the newspaper I worked for when I covered the Bulls, for accurate statistical and anecdotal information.

Because the dynasty Bulls were such a big story, they were regularly covered as well by the magazines *Sports Illustrated* and *Sporting News*. I found issues in library archives and plummed them for information.

The following is a list of books and websites I also used to provide information for this book:

Condor, Bob. *Michael Jordan's 50 Greatest Games: from His NCAA Championship to Six NBA Titles*. Secaucus, NJ: Carol Pub. Group, 1998. Print.

Jackson, Phil, and Charles Rosen. *More than a Game*. New York: Seven Stories, 2001. Print.

Jackson, Phil, and Hugh Delehanty. *Sacred Hoops: Spiritual Lessons of a Hardwood Warrior*. New York: Hyperion, 1995. Print.

Kerr, Johnny, and Terry Pluto. *Bull Session: an Up-close Look at Michael Jordan and Courtside Stories about the Chicago Bulls*. Chicago: Bonus, 1989. Print.

LaBlanc, Michael L., and Mary K. Ruby. *Basketball*. Detroit: Gale Research, 1994. Print.

Lazenby, Roland. *Blood on the Horns: the Long Strange Ride of Michael Jordan's Chicago Bulls*. Lenexa, KS: Addax Pub. Group, 1998. Print.

Lazenby, Roland. *Mindgames: Phil Jackson's Long, Strange Journey*. Lincolnwood, IL: Contemporary, 2001. Print.

Lazenby, Roland. *Bull Run!: The Story of the 1995-96 Chicago Bulls: The Greatest Team in Basketball History*. Lenexa, Kan.: Addax Pub. Group, 1996. Print.

Lazenby, Roland. *And Now, Your Chicago Bulls!: a Thirty-year Celebration!* Dallas, TX: Taylor Pub., 1995. Print.

Sachare, Alex. *The Chicago Bulls Encyclopedia*. Lincolnwood, IL: Contemporary, 1999. Print.

Smith, Sam. *The Jordan Rules*. New York: Simon and Schuster, 1992. Print.

Wennington, Bill, and Kent McDill. *Bill Wennington's Tales from the Bulls Hardwood*. Champaign, IL: Sports Pub., 2004. Print.

www.nba.com/bulls
www.basketball-reference.com
www.teamusa.org
www.sweetspeeches.com
www.imdb.com
www.espnchicago.com

About The Author

Kent McDill was going to be a broadcaster, but along the way somebody decided he could write and turned him into a newspaperman.

After graduating with a communications degree from DePauw University in 1978, McDill was hired by United Press International (UPI) to be a broadcast sportswriter for television and radio, stationed in his hometown of Chicago. In 1980, UPI asked him to become the Indiana state sports editor for the newspaper division. He made his decision to accept the move to Indianapolis based on the knowledge that by taking the job he would get to meet tennis star Chris Evert, which he did.

In 1985, McDill was transferred back to Chicago, where he eventually became the Midwest sports editor, in charge of sports coverage for eight states. In 1988, the *Daily Herald* of Arlington Heights decided to start sending reporters on the road with the pro teams from Chicago, and hired McDill to be the Bulls beat writer.

McDill traveled with the Bulls from 1988 to 1999, and was the only beat writer to cover all six of the Bulls championship teams.

In 1999, McDill began covering both the Chicago Bears and Chicago Fire for the *Herald*. In 2008, he resigned from the *Herald* to become a freelancer, but in 2009 he was back on the Bulls beat, this time for nba.com.

McDill and his wife, Janice, have four children: Haley, Dan, Lindsey, and Kyle.